I0833495

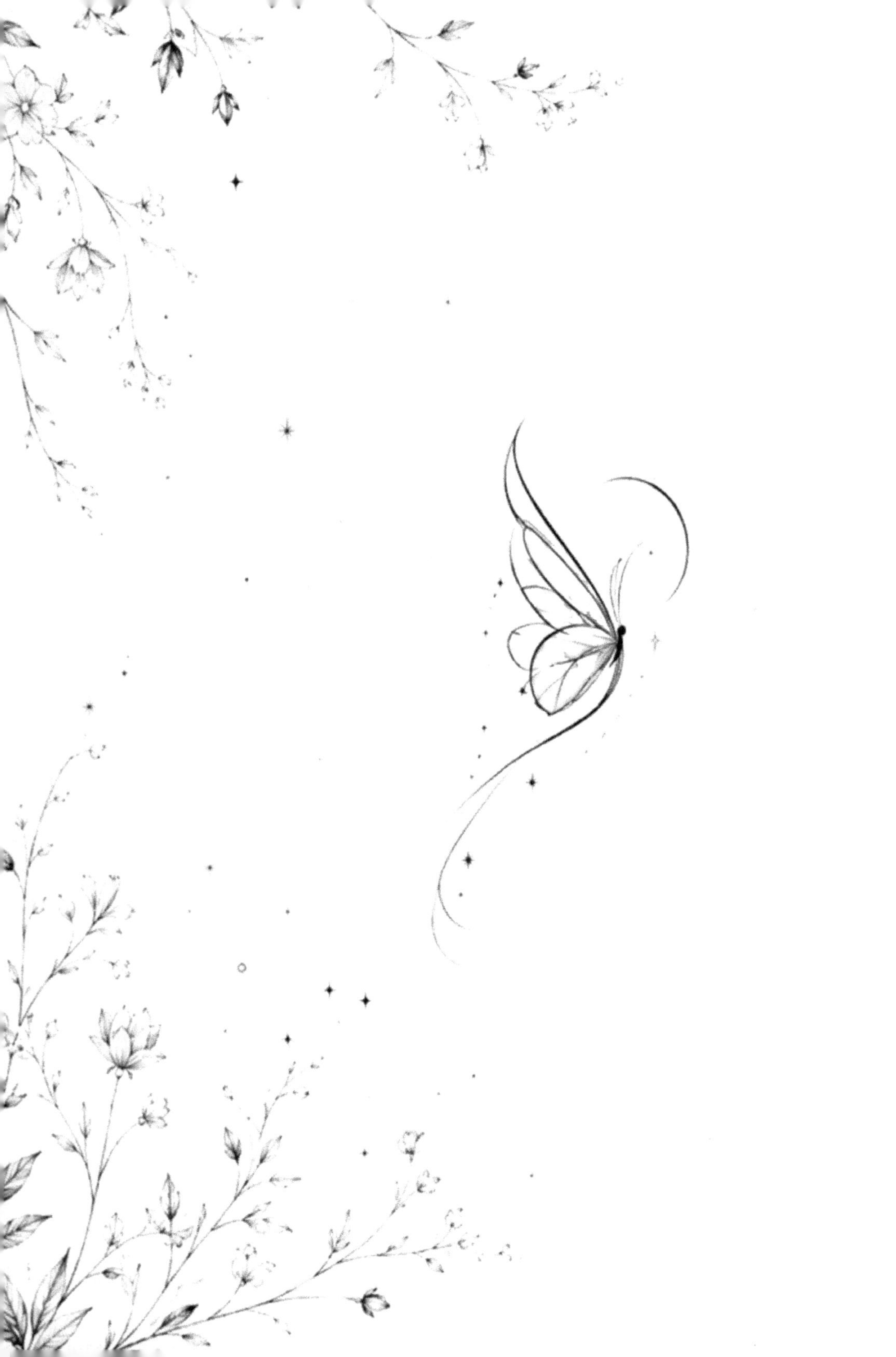

BY
DR. PATTI MILLS

Dedication

I would like to dedicate this book to all the present and retired educators in my family: Aretha, Anthony, Bleston, Jem, Natalia, Treasure, and Joshua. May God's grace continue to guide, strengthen, and bless each of them always.

Acknowledgment

I would like to acknowledge my children—Natalia, Barrington, and Marcilyn—and my husband, Robert.

They are proof that a person who has had a bad childhood can indeed produce children who are well-balanced mentally.

I love and appreciate each of them for understanding me and showing me love and appreciation.

About the Author

Dr. Patti Mills has been an Educator for the past 24 years. She obtained her Bachelor's, Master's, and Doctorate degrees from Nova Southeastern University. Dr. Mills is also a realtor and an Author.

Dr. Mills is a Jamaican by birth but a naturalized American citizen who has resided in the United States for 40-plus years. She is married and has three wonderful children: Natalia, an Educator; Barrington, a Law Enforcement Officer; Marcilyn, a Pharmacist; and her husband, Robert.

Prologue

It is reputed that the first formative years of a child's life are crucial to their upbringing. This premise might be debatable, but research does, in fact, indicate that this is true. The irony is that a child who has a traumatic early childhood does not necessarily turn out to be a problem for society; many survive with healthy lives with or without professional assistance. The rationale for this might be related to the resilience they were born with. The fact is, an individual can survive with a fulfilling life without any influence from their traumatic childhood.

Contents

Dedication i

Acknowledgment ii

About the Author iii

Prologue iv

Chapter 1: The Child Left in the Shadows 1

Chapter 2: Faith in the Unfaithful 9

Chapter 3: The Countryside 31

Chapter 4: My Saving Grace 42

Chapter 5: The Fate of Elaina 55

Chapter 6: A New Life 70

Chapter 7: My First School Escapades 84

Chapter 8: Events Before My Father's Return 89

Chapter 9: The Last Years with Viv and My Father 95

Chapter 10: My Emergence into Adulthood 101

Chapter 11: My Work Life Before USA 107

Chapter 12: My First Two Years in the USA – Chicago, Illinois 112

Chapter 13: My Relocation to Miami, Florida 118

Epilogue......122

Chapter 1: The Child Left in the Shadows

I was born in a place full of music, but I grew up without a song of my own.

My name is Elaina, and I came into this world in Kingston, Jamaica.

I was only 8 years old, though I did not know what years meant. All I knew was the yard outside our house, the street that was full of voices and bright laughter, and the air that always seemed like it was coming from a huge heater.

When I was a child, mornings followed a familiar pattern. The roosters cried at first light, pulling everyone from sleep. Pots clattered in nearby kitchens, and the scent of dumplings slipped in through the open windows. These sounds and smells greeted me before I stirred from bed. Whenever I got to step out, the ground felt warm beneath my bare feet. People talked and laughed like there was no tomorrow.

Silence was a stranger to Kingston.

The roofs shimmered under the burning sun, and the streets glowed under the moonlight. Whether it was day or night, the air was alive with sound—drums in the distance or calypso music drifting from a radio. Children ran down the lane, their laughter following behind them. The women on the corner babbled, their voices strong like the peppers they sold. The men played dominoes at the rum shop and slammed the tiles so hard the sound reached our house.

To me, the city was both wide and small. Wide, because there was always more noise, more colors, more things happening beyond the gate. Small, because most of the time I only watched. I stood at the edge of our yard, clutching the fence, wishing I could follow the children down the street, wishing someone would call me to join them.

Because I knew, deep inside, that I could not have a childhood like kids my age were getting all around me…

I felt like an outsider, like I didn't belong and was mistakenly brought into this world. I felt it again one night, as I sat in the doorway, knees pulled to my chest, watching Ryan and Jezzy, my half-brother and half-sister, getting ready to go to a party I was not allowed to attend. My eyes followed the way Jezzy was shining with excitement, the way Ryan kept doing a little dance as he got ready.

Ryan stood in front of the small, cracked mirror, his hands smoothing his shirt collar over and over again. He looked at his reflection with a deep focus, as if a single wrong fold might keep him from being let inside the party.

"Jezzy, give me the comb!" he said, tilting his chin toward the dresser.

Jezzy, already in her new dress, spun once in a little circle before she handed it to him. The fabric of her dress swished around her legs. "You always brush your hair too much," she teased, her voice sweet and light, but with a sharp little edge at the end.

"No, I don't!" Ryan protested, running the comb through his short curls. "I just want it to be flat."

Jezzy laughed. Her laughter was a bright, clear sound that filled the small room. I watched her from my corner as she slid her feet into her new shoes. She gently patted the shiny black leather, as if it were the most precious treasure in the world.

Then she groaned.

"These hurt."

"Then don't wear them," Ryan said simply, still looking at his reflection.

"I want to." Jezzy pouted. "They're pretty."

"Pretty silly," Ryan said.

Jezzy made a face at him. "You're silly."

As the two talked, I stayed quiet, just watching them. I loved these moments, when they were so wrapped up in their own little world that they forgot I was there. Their easy laughter and quick back-and-forth jokes felt like a secret language I didn't know. I just tried to catch the little pieces of their joy that floated through the air, hold them for myself, and pretend I was part of it all.

I wanted to ask what the party would be like. Would the music sound like the drums I sometimes heard drifting from the streets? Would the food taste as sweet as the fried dumplings that filled the mornings? But the words stayed inside me. I already knew the answer. The party was not mine to imagine.

Mama.

Jezzy leaned close to the mirror and smeared a bit of her mama's lip balm on her mouth. "Do you think Mama will come with us?" she asked, watching Ryan through the mirror.

"She has to," Ryan said, tugging at his sleeves. "I'm not getting my new shoes all dirty in the mud."

For them, it meant Viv, the woman I called stepmother. For me, it meant someone else, someone gone too soon. I hugged my knees tighter, pressing my chin down, letting their voices roll past me.

I stayed that way, silent, watching, wishing, knowing.

At some point, Jezzy's eyes lifted from the mirror and found my curled-up form. She stopped brushing her hair for a moment, the bristles hanging in the air. She tilted her head slightly, and the playful teasing on her face softened into something different. She set the brush down and walked over to me, her new dress rustling with every step she took.

"Elaina," she said, her voice dropping to a whisper. She crouched down so we were eye to eye. "I'm so sorry you can't come with us tonight."

I didn't say anything. Just stared at my feet.

Jezzy bit down on her lip, her expression caught somewhere between worry and kindness. Her fingers worked at something bright in her hand, turning it carefully as if it might slip away. She leaned closer and extended her hand. A ribbon appeared between us, pale pink and soft, lined with the most delicate flowers stitched along its edge.

"Here. You can wear this," she said kindly, her eyes darting here and there, "It's not much, but it's pretty, isn't it?" Her gesture surprised me, because she was always mean to me.

My chest felt like it was fluttering with a million tiny butterflies. I reached out with both hands, taking the ribbon as if it were a priceless jewel. It seemed to glow in the dim lamplight, softer and more beautiful than anything I had ever owned. For a second, I completely forgot about the loud music outside, the fancy dresses I couldn't have, and the doors always closed.

For that moment, I felt like I belonged in their world.

I pressed the ribbon against my cheek. "Thank you, Jezzy. It's so beautiful," I whispered, my eyes almost welling up from the emotions in my throat.

But before I could even try to tie it in my hair, another hand—larger, stronger, colder—swooped down and snatched the ribbon right out of my grasp.

"Mama..." Jezzy pleaded, but it was too late.

My stepmother was standing over us, her tall shadow falling over us. Her eyes darted from Jezzy's guilty face to my own, which I knew was filled with a childish hope that she hated. A smile that didn't reach her eyes appeared on her lips.

"That girl needs no ribbons in her life," she said, her voice sweet but sharp like a knife. She yanked Jezzy up to her side and turned on her heel. "Come. You'll ruin your dress fussing over her."

The ribbon dangled in Viv's hand as she pulled my sister away, and I watched until they disappeared down the hall.

I stayed where I was, my palms still open, still warm from holding the gift that was no longer mine.

It wasn't the first time Viv had taken something from me. She had long ago decided I was not to go where her children went. I had no dresses, because she refused to buy me any. I had no shoes for dancing, no books for learning. When Ryan and Jezzy went to school, I stayed behind and was left to sweep the floors or fetch water.

Viv never tried to do even the simplest things for me. She didn't wash my clothes, so I wore them until they were stiff and rough against my skin. She didn't comb my hair, letting it tangle into knots that hurt when I tried to pull them out with my fingers. Sometimes, I would watch her fuss over Jezzy's curls, smoothing them with sweet-smelling oil, and I would wonder what it might feel like to have someone's gentle hands touch my head like that.

But I never asked. I already knew the answer.

In Viv's house, I was always the one left behind.

Ryan and Jezzy stood by the front door, their faces bright with excitement. They were now dressed and ready to go. They talked over each other, a rush of words about who they hoped to see at the party. Ryan insisted some of his school friends, including a few guys from his football team, would be there. Jezzy just laughed and quickly listed the names of the girls she hoped to see, detailing what each one would probably be wearing.

My stepmother stepped forward and knelt, her eyes focused only on Jezzy. She carefully smoothed the fabric of Jezzy's dress, her hands moving with a gentleness that only a mother could carry. She adjusted the bow at her back, making sure it sat perfectly. She reached up and gently brushed a stray strand of hair from Jezzy's face, tucking it behind her ear.

All the while, she smiled, nodding along as Jezzy chattered on, though I knew she wasn't truly listening. Her hands stayed busy, checking every tiny detail of the dress and her hair before she finally stepped back.

"You look absolutely lovely," Viv said to Jezzy, a wide, proud smile stretching across her face.

Then, almost as an afterthought, she glanced at Ryan. She straightened his collar and then waved them both toward the door. "Go on now. Don't be late."

The children rushed out, a burst of energy, their voices and laughter spilling into the street. They ran toward the party just two blocks away, a place I couldn't go. I watched them go, two bright figures getting smaller and smaller until they turned a corner and were gone.

An immeasurable silence filled the house.

I stood in my corner, hoping to be forgotten, to melt back into the shadows where I belonged. But my stepmother, Viv, turned from the door. Her eyes, which had been so soft and full of pride as she watched Jezzy, became hard and sharp when they landed on me. The smile she had worn just a moment ago vanished completely.

"What are you looking at?" she snapped, her voice cutting through the stillness like a knife. "Go and clean the kitchen now."

She didn't wait for me to move. She just turned her back and walked away, her footsteps disappearing down the hall until the door to her own room clicked shut. That small sound sealed me into the silence. I knew I couldn't waste a second. If she came back and found me still standing there, she would punish me. That was how it always worked. I had no one to speak up for me, no one to tell her to stop. I was just a child, too small and too scared to fight against her rules.

The rag slipped into my hand slowly, as though even my body resisted the task. My thoughts stayed on the party, the music that pulsed, the bright lights that burned, and the children's laughter that excluded me.

A deep sadness filled my chest, heavy and unspoken. I sank to my knees beside the pots and scrubbed them clean, but my thoughts strayed far away. Still, the sounds traveled to me—the echo of laughter, the hum of a song drifting down the street. It felt close enough to touch, but I could not reach it. I caught myself longing for silence, if only to free my mind from what it could not have.

I thought about my real mother, the woman I only remembered in bits and pieces. Would she have combed my hair like Viv did for Jezzy? Would she have smiled at me the way she smiled at her own children? I did not know, and it hurt to think about it. I often wondered where my place in the world was. It never felt like it was here, in this house where I was seen but never cared for, where I was told what to do but never asked what I wanted. I was a girl in a home full of people, but no one to stand with me.

The kitchen floor was cold under my knees, and the water grew colder as I worked. I scrubbed harder, trying to wash away the lonely feeling inside me. I wished I could find a place where I truly belonged, where my laughter could be as bright as Jezzy's, and someone could be proud of me. I kept scrubbing, watching the water turn gray with dirt, wishing the dirt could take away the emptiness in my heart.

When the house was empty and I was left with my own thoughts, I tried to hold on to the faces I thought were my own. My father, Robert.

And my mother, Ruth.

Chapter 2: Faith in the Unfaithful

10 years ago, something special happened.

Robert first saw Ruth on a warm Sunday afternoon in Kingston.

The market was noisy, and the stalls were crowded with people selling mangoes, plantains, and yams. Women called out their prices while children weaved through the crowd carrying baskets. The air was teeming with the smell of roasted corn and fresh bread.

Robert had come with his older cousin to help carry home goods, but his eyes kept moving across the busy square—eyes that never seemed to rest.

That was when he noticed Ruth, standing by a stall of ripe oranges.

She wore a simple blue dress, her hair tied back neatly, and her hands moved gently as she picked through the fruit. Something about her quiet grace caught his attention.

Robert's cousin nudged him. "Why're you staring so hard, man?" he teased.

Robert laughed but could not look away. "I've never seen someone like her before," he said softly.

As Ruth turned to pay the vendor, her eyes lifted and met his. It was only for a moment, but she offered a small smile before turning back to her basket. Robert felt his heart beat faster, and before he could stop himself, he walked toward her.

"Good afternoon," he said, his voice polite but nervous.

Ruth looked at him with surprise, then nodded.

"Afternoon."

He pointed to the oranges in her basket. "You choose the sweetest ones," he said. "My mother always says the ones with the brightest skin taste best."

Ruth's lips curved into a smile. "Then your mother is right," she replied. "These are for her?"

"No," Robert said quickly, shaking his head. "She sent me here to help my cousin. But I think I came for something else too."

Ruth tilted her head. "And what is that?"

Robert hesitated, then spoke with a boldness that surprised even him. "To meet you."

Ruth held back her words, choosing instead to look directly at him, her eyes restless and probing. The market continued in its bustle, yet the noise seemed to lose its edge, fading until it no longer reached them. A low, musical laugh rose from her, not loud, but filled with the uneasy charm of a feeling she could not hide.

"You are very sure of yourself."

Robert grinned. "Not sure. Just hopeful."

***

Their first date went amazingly.

Robert had asked Ruth if she would walk with him the following Sunday after church. She agreed with a shy nod, and all week, Robert could not think of anything else.

That Sunday, the streets were quieter than on the weekday market. The sun was warm but gentle, and the sea breeze carried the smell of salt through the air. Ruth wore a white dress with small flowers stitched near the collar. Robert wore his best shirt, freshly ironed, though he kept pulling at the sleeves to make sure it sat right.

They walked side by side down a narrow lane that led toward the water. Children played marbles in the dust, and an old man strummed a guitar under a tree. Robert glanced at Ruth every few steps, still amazed she had agreed to meet him.

"You walk fast," Robert said with a small laugh, trying to hide his nerves.

Ruth smiled. "You just walk slow."

Her voice was playful, and Robert relaxed. "Maybe I walk slow because I want the day to last longer," he replied.

She looked at him then, her eyes bright in the sunlight. "You have many words, don't you?"

"Not many," Robert said. "Only the ones I mean."

They reached the shore where the waves touched the sand in soft curls. The water sparkled, and a group of fishermen pulled in their nets while shouting to one another. Robert and Ruth sat on a large rock, their shoulders almost touching. For a moment, neither of them spoke, the sound of the sea filling the silence.

Ruth was the first to break it. "Why did you really come to me that day at the market?"

Robert took a breath. "Because I felt something," he said simply. "I cannot explain it. I just knew I should not let you walk away without a word."

Ruth lowered her gaze, her fingers tracing the hem of her dress. "I thought you were too forward," she admitted, then smiled. "But maybe that is what I liked."

The sun dipped lower, painting the sky in soft gold. Robert wished time could stop, that the day could stay frozen with Ruth beside him and the sea stretching out forever. As they rose to leave, he dared to reach for her hand. She did not pull away.

***

A week later, Ruth noticed small changes in her body.

One morning, she woke up before the rooster like she always did, but this time her stomach lurched the moment she stepped outside. She clutched the basin, her body trembling as a bitter taste rose in her throat.

The sickness returned the next day, and the day after, until she could no longer pretend it was nothing. When her monthly time failed to come, she realized what was really happening.

She was carrying a child.

As soon as she found out, she hid herself in her room, thinking over and over about this unexpected discovery. She was confused, for she both felt nervous and excited. Nervous because she was young and unmarried and knew the whispers that followed women of this kind. Excited, because the child was Robert's.

It was some nights after their first date, when she gave herself to him, and he left his seed within her.

Ruth rested her hand on her belly and smiled to herself. For all her fears, she was glad it was his child she carried. Robert had been nothing but sweet with her, always attentive, always lifting her spirit. In his presence, she felt safe and cherished, as if she were the most beautiful woman in the whole of Jamaica.

Little did she know Robert was only half the man she believed him to be.

***

Ruth knew the day she would tell Robert the news—Sunday. He would be there, just like he always was. Her sweaty hands clenched her basket as she searched for Robert in the crowd of busybodies, her heart racing with each dart of her eye.

She spotted him near the fruit stall. He looked much the same, but something felt different. His eyes wandered, his smile faint and hollow. When he noticed her, he gave only a small nod instead of the warm greeting she had hoped for. Ruth's chest tightened, but she forced a smile and went to him.

"Good morning, Robert," she said softly.

"Morning," he replied, his tone flat. His gaze drifted past her, toward the crowd, as if he were searching for someone else.

Ruth tried to speak of small things, the mangoes, the price of bread, the smell of roasted corn in the air, yet every word seemed to fall against a wall. Robert answered politely, but there was no spark in his voice, none of the laughter that once came so easily.

Her palms grew damp around the basket handle. She had pictured this moment many times, imagined the joy in his eyes, the way he might take her hand and promise they would face everything together. Instead, doubt began to gnaw at her. She wondered if she should remain silent, if perhaps the market was the wrong place or time.

Robert turned down a narrow, more private lane than the market. Ruth followed, still uncertain. The noise of the crowd gradually disappeared behind them. He stopped near a shaded corner, leaning against a wall with his arms crossed. His face was calm, but there was something wrong with his eyes. They seemed…dull.

Ruth stood before him, gathering her courage. She had to tell him.

"Robert," she began, her voice trembling, "there is something I need to tell you."

His eyes found hers at last, and the suddenness of it struck her with a force she had not expected. The shock sent her heart rising painfully into her throat, and she was left struggling against the weight of her own breath. Her fingers clung to the basket, turning and twisting the edge as though by that small act she might keep from falling apart.

"I am pregnant," she whispered. "It is yours."

For a moment, something dark crossed Robert's eyes. It was quick but strong enough to make Ruth's skin prickle. She almost stepped back; certain she had seen fear or anger flicker there. Then it was gone, hidden as if it had never been. His mouth curved into a smile, his voice gentle, calm, and full of false warmth.

"That is wonderful news, Ruth," he said, stepping closer. His hands touched her shoulders before drawing her into his arms. His cheek rested against her hair as if nothing had unsettled him at all.

Closing her eyes, Ruth released a slow breath while her basket shifted loosely at her side. "I was so nervous to tell you," She whispered. "But I knew you would be happy."

"I am happy," Robert murmured, his hand sliding across her back. "Everything will be all right."

Her lips lifted into a smile as she leaned against him. All her worry seemed to fall away in that embrace. She believed every word, and the secret she had carried with such fear now felt like a promise of joy.

What she didn't know was that, on the same day, another woman had come to tell him that he had impregnated her.

***

Ruth lived in a dream that was never real, and her faith in Robert only grew when he asked her to move in with him. She was overjoyed; certain he wanted to build a home with her, make her his wife, and raise the child she carried. To her, it was proof of his love and devotion.

In truth, Robert was hiding from his *other* problem, or the other woman he had gotten pregnant. Moving in with Ruth gave him the perfect cover. He wore the mask of a loving partner while quietly pushing aside the life he had created elsewhere, all while Ruth remained blind to the betrayal unfolding beside her.

Almost chirping with excitement, Ruth moved into Robert's house, confident that he was a good man prepared to take responsibility. Her pregnancy did not trouble her. She saw no shame in it and never considered the child a burden. The thought of sharing a home with Robert made her believe she had secured her future, that he would soon become the husband she longed for and the father her child deserved.

The days inside those walls told a different story.

Robert was not the partner she had imagined. He spent long hours sunk in silence; his gaze fixed on some distance only he could see. When Ruth prepared meals with care, he ate without comment, sometimes pushing his food aside untouched. She brought flowers to the table, smoothed the sheets, and folded their clothes neatly into the wooden chest, but nothing seemed to stir warmth from him. The house echoed with the sounds of her effort, while Robert glided like a shadow through the rooms, thorn with the guilt that another woman was also carrying his child.

She suspected that there might have been another woman, but forced it away if a sliver of doubt touched her, clinging harder to the story she wanted to believe. Her heart needed him to be the man she had dreamed of, because she was carrying his child and could not bear the thought of facing the truth alone.

***

Ruth had been in labor through the night, her cries filling the small house. The midwife repeatedly wiped her brow, whispering encouragement, urging her to push. Robert walked the floor outside, his hands clenching and unclenching, his face pale. He knew what was happening in that room was his doing, and he also knew another woman, somewhere else, carried his child as well. The thought gnawed at him even as he waited for the sound of Ruth's labor to end.

When the first cry pierced the air, Robert froze. The sharp, raw voice of new life rang in his ears, and his chest tightened. He stepped into the doorway just as the midwife placed the small, wriggling body on Ruth's chest.

Ruth lay spent, her hair damp, her face glowing with relief. Tears slid down her cheeks as she whispered, “She is beautiful.” Her voice trembled with awe.

Moving with hesitation and care, Robert approached the bed as if it might explode at any moment. He looked at the tiny face, the clenched fists, the fragile body pressed against Ruth, and forced a smile onto his lips. He touched the baby’s hand, and his breath caught when her fingers closed around his.

“Our daughter,” he said softly, as though the words might anchor him in the moment.

“Yes, Robert. Our daughter.” Ruth’s eyes shone as she gazed at him.

The midwife wrapped the child and returned her to Ruth’s arms. Robert pulled a chair beside the bed and sat close, his eyes fixed on the baby. To Ruth, his silence might have seemed full of meaning, but it was the silence of a man holding back more than he revealed.

He reached for the blanket and smoothed it over the infant. His smile stayed a tad bit longer than it could be deemed natural.

“She will have my strength,” he murmured, then glanced at Ruth, “and your heart.”

Ruth laughed weakly, clutching the baby close.

“Whatever she has, she is ours.”

The night outside was still, the stars hidden by clouds. Inside, Ruth believed everything had changed for the better.

Robert knew differently. Another child would soon arrive, one he had no intention of claiming so openly.

***

One month later, Robert's other child, Dora, was born.

Robert left them both behind, but got in touch when Dora got older.

Those early months were quiet for me, pretty different from how most babies act. Ruth, who was my mom by then, would hold me tight against her. She'd rock back and forth, singing soft little songs that felt like a warm blanket. Her singing wasn't perfect like the radio stars, but I bet it was the best thing I'd ever heard.

I hardly ever cried unless I was hungry. She could do her housework with me right there. People who stopped by would look at me and say I seemed like an old spirit. They noticed how I kept my eyes wide open, always looking around like I knew stuff other babies didn't.

Robert, my father, wasn't big on showing feelings, but we knew he cared about me. When I was tiny, he had his own way of caring without saying much or touching. He'd sit there watching me from the other side of the room, his eyes getting a bit softer—something only my mother picked up on. He didn't talk much, but you could tell he cared by the little stuff, like making sure we had enough of everything or taking an extra minute before heading to work.

Ruth loved seeing that and kept it close. It made her day knowing he cared about me, even if he was quiet about it. She'd kiss my face over and over, put ribbons in my hair, and tell me bedtime stories until I fell asleep. She'd whisper, "You're my blessing," and when she smiled, I felt protected. Her hands had that mix of soap and cooking smells. The house finally felt peaceful, and it looked like nothing would mess that up...

...then Viv showed up a few months later.

***

Viv was a young woman living near my mother and father. People in the neighborhood knew her not for kindness, but for the trouble she often left behind. Her words were sharp, and she seemed to take pleasure in finding faults in others. If someone walked by with a smile, she would find a reason to sour it. When children laughed in the street, she scolded them as if their joy was an insult to her.

In the market, she pushed her way forward, snatching the best fruits before anyone else could reach them. If a neighbor asked for help, she acted as though the request was beneath her. She was never generous with her time or her heart. Some said she was clever, but it was a cleverness used for twisting truth, spreading rumors, and turning people against one another.

Her house was filled with things she had gathered for herself, but it never felt warm or welcoming. She liked control, and she liked seeing others bend to her will. Even small victories, such as making someone uneasy with a single glance, gave her a sense of triumph.

Viv was not beautiful, but she carried herself as if she were. She knew how to twist a glance and soften her voice until it sounded sweet, though it was only a mask. Beneath that false charm was coldness, a hunger to take what belonged to others, and a restless spite that never allowed her peace.

On one fateful day, her scheming eyes landed on my father.

She watched him from across the street as he worked outside, fixing something near the fence. His shirt clung to him in the heat, his face calm and focused. Viv's lips curved into a smile that was far from innocent.

"That one," she whispered to herself. "He will be mine."

The thought thrilled her. Not love stirred in her, but a sharp desire to take what was not hers. She knew he had a woman, my mother, but she did not care. To her, that only made the challenge sweeter. She enjoyed tearing apart what others held dear, as if destroying happiness gave her more power.

Later that day, Viv crossed paths with him on purpose. She walked slowly, letting her dress sway, her face painted with a smile that pretended kindness.

"Good afternoon," she called out in a voice softer than silk.

My father, unaware of her schemes, looked up from his work.

"Afternoon," he said politely, brushing the dust from his hands.

Viv tilted her head. "You're always working so hard. A man like you should be appreciated. Not many could handle a house like this on their own."

He gave her a small smile, the kind he offered to anyone in passing. "It's nothing. Just keeping things in order."

Viv stepped closer, her eyes narrowing in interest. "Still, it's impressive. A strong man deserves recognition. Some people do not always see what they have."

My father raised a brow, not quite sure what she meant, but he only nodded and turned back to his work. He already had enough on his plate. He didn't want any more trouble. However, Viv's smile did not fade. If anything, it deepened, as though his indifference only made her more determined.

As she walked away, she muttered under her breath, "You'll see me again. And next time, you won't look away so quickly."

***

Viv immediately acted by finding out the route my father took to and from work. For days, she lingered at corners, pretending to shop, pretending to chat, all while watching carefully. She memorized the times he left the house, the streets he preferred, and the pauses he made along the way. Once she knew his routine, she began her game.

The first time she stepped into his path, she clutched a basket filled with bread. As he approached, she let one loaf slip, rolling across the dirt.

"Oh no!" she cried, bending down with exaggerated distress.

My father stopped and picked it up before she could reach it.

"Here," he said simply, placing it back into her basket.

Her smile was bright, her eyes soft. "How kind of you. Always a gentleman."

He nodded and continued walking, but she had planted the seed. The second meeting came a week later, this time near the small market. She appeared as though she had just finished shopping, her arms full, and when she saw him, she sighed.

"These bags are heavier than I thought. Would you mind walking a little with me?"

He hesitated, then agreed, carrying one basket for her. She filled the silence with stories, laughter that rang louder than necessary, and small compliments that slipped between her words.

"Not many men are as helpful as you," she said, glancing at him from under her lashes. "Your wife is very lucky."

He gave no reply, his expression unreadable, but Viv caught the faintest flicker of pride in his eyes. That was enough for her.

Slowly, slowly, she continued. Each "accidental" meeting felt natural on the surface, but underneath was careful planning. She made sure she was always in his path, always at the right time, always ready with a smile or a remark that lingered in his mind.

And my father, though strong and quiet, began to pause when he saw her. He listened a little longer and answered her questions with more words than before.

Without even realizing it, he was taking small steps into her trap.

***

At first, my mother thought Robert was beginning to change for the better. He came home on time, sat with her on the porch, and even asked small questions about her day. For a little while, it seemed as if he was trying to be the man she hoped he would become. Then, almost without warning, the warmth faded. He returned later and later, brushing off her questions with clipped replies. When she tried to share her stories, his eyes drifted elsewhere, his nods empty, his mind far from her words.

One evening, she placed dinner on the table, the same stew she knew he liked. He took a few bites, then pushed the plate away with a sigh.

"Not hungry," he muttered.

Her eyes followed him as he rose and left the room, his shoulders tense, his gaze fixed anywhere but on her. She sat quietly, her spoon resting in the bowl, wondering what had come between them.

My mother felt dismayed. Just when Robert had begun to show signs of being better for her and for me, Elaina, he took a sharp step back. She grew determined to mend whatever was slipping away. At night, she reached for his hand beneath the blanket, hoping he would hold on. Instead, he pulled away.

Her voice broke as she whispered, "Is something wrong?"

His answer came flat and lifeless. "No, nothing's wrong. Just tired."

He turned his back and drifted into sleep, leaving her wide awake in the silence. Tears slid into her pillow as she sobbed quietly, careful not to wake him. In her heart, she already knew. There was another woman.

***

Soon, when I turned six months old, the straw broke the camel's back.

My father came home one evening, his face set in a way my mother had never seen before. He sat down at the table, his hands folded tightly together, as if bracing himself. My mother wiped her hands on her apron and looked at him with quiet concern.

"What is it?" she asked.

He lifted his eyes, and the words came out flat. "I found someone."

The air in the room seemed to stop. My mother blinked, certain she had misheard. "What do you mean?" Her voice cracked with disbelief.

"I have met someone else," he said, avoiding her gaze. "It has been some time now. I cannot hide it anymore."

Her hands gripped the edge of the table. "You're telling me this while our child is still in my arms? After everything we built?"

He shifted uncomfortably, his eyes dark. "I did not plan for it to happen. But it did. I cannot ignore it."

Her breath caught, her chest tight. She shook her head over and over, refusing to accept the words spilling from his mouth. "No. You don't mean that. You're tired. You're confused. This is your home, your family. We are your family."

He stood up, his chair scraping the floor. "I am sorry," he said, though there was no real meaning behind his words.

***

Ruth had never known anger like this before. It burned through her veins, sharp and alive, when Robert admitted there was another woman. She refused to sit by and watch him slip away without a fight. If he thought he could fool around while she stayed silent, he was wrong. She would see for herself.

On Saturday afternoon, as Robert dressed to leave, Ruth stood in the doorway with me in her arms.

"I am coming with you," she said.

His head snapped up. "No, Ruth. Not today."

Her grip on me tightened, her eyes hard. "I said I am coming."

The argument rose quickly, his voice sharp, hers relentless. In the end, he gave in, though his lips were pressed thin with annoyance. Together they stepped into the street, Ruth clutching me close as if I were her shield.

Robert's walk was strange, almost aimless. He changed lanes often, paused at corners too long, and glanced back over his shoulder as though uncertain of where he was going. Ruth watched him with suspicion. He was not leading her anywhere; he was avoiding it.

The market welcomed them with thick air, laden with ripe fruit and salted fish smells. Robert bent over a stall, choosing oranges with deliberate care, when a voice rang out behind him.

"Robert, why didn't you come?"

Ruth stiffened. Viv stood only a few steps away, her eyes bright with triumph. She wore her smile like a blade, sharp and mocking. Her gaze shifted to Ruth, and that smile deepened into something almost cruel.

"So this is why," Viv said softly, as if tasting the words. "You bring her here."

Ruth's heart thudded against her ribs. She knew without being told. This was the other woman. She drew me tighter against her chest, her jaw set, her eyes locked on Viv's face.

Viv tilted her head, amusement curling her lips. "Poor little woman trying to be his wife," she murmured. "Still holding on, are you?"

No word escaped Ruth's lips, but the fury gathered like a storm in her silence. The hard light of her stare told Viv everything she needed to know. She would not stoop to shouting; she denied her that victory. With me pressed against her, she rooted herself to the ground, her strength showing in restraint rather than in noise.

Viv stepped closer, her tone sharper. "You should learn when to let go. Men like Robert do not belong to women like you."

Ruth's breath came fast, her body trembling, but she did not flinch. Her eyes stayed fixed on Viv.

The tension split when Robert turned, his face flushed with rage.

"Enough," he barked, his voice cracking through the air. "Both of you. Stop this."

But at that moment, something dark took hold of Viv. Her dislike for Ruth burned hotter than before, sharpened by jealousy. Ruth was far prettier than she was, with her long, flowing hair and graceful figure, and that beauty only deepened Viv's resentment. What began as rivalry hardened into hatred—a hatred rooted in envy and pride.

***

Their next meeting did not happen by chance. Viv made certain of it. She lingered near the lane Ruth often walked, waiting with her arms folded and her eyes sharp. When Ruth appeared, carrying me against her hip with a cloth bag balanced on the other arm, Viv stepped out from the shadows of the alley.

"So there she is," Viv drawled, her lips curling. "The little mother who thinks she's won."

Ruth tensed up but kept walking, her chin lifted, her steps steady. She had no wish to quarrel. "Leave me be, Viv. I have nothing to say to you."

Viv laughed, the sound low and mocking. "Oh, you have plenty to say. You just don't have the courage. Do you think Robert will stay with you forever? Do you think that baby will keep him from me?"

Ruth stopped, her jaw tightening. "He is not yours to take," she said, her voice shaking with quiet fury. "And you will not speak of my child."

Viv's eyes narrowed. She took a step closer until their faces nearly met. "Robert was mine the moment I wanted him," she hissed. "And everything of yours, I will take too."

The air between them changed with tension. Ruth shifted me higher on her hip, freeing her right hand. Viv noticed the movement and smirked, mistaking it for weakness.

Without warning, she lunged.

The women grappled in the dust of the road. Ruth tried to shield me while striking out with her free hand. Viv clawed at her, her voice spitting curses, determined to destroy the beauty she was so jealous of. Neighbors shouted from their doorways, but none dared step between them.

Ruth raised her hand to push Viv away. In a sudden frenzy, Viv seized her fingers and sank her teeth hard. Ruth screamed, the sound tearing through the street, as Viv bit through the tip of her index finger. Blood welled instantly, streaking down Ruth's hand and onto her dress.

"You devil!" Ruth cried, clutching her ruined hand to her chest while still trying to keep me safe in her arms.

But it was done.

Viv had won.

***

It was only one of many troubles. Viv did not stop after biting Ruth's finger. Each day, she grew bolder. She followed Ruth in the market. She shouted cruel words in the street. Sometimes she came near the house late at night, her voice loud with anger, making the neighbors whisper. Ruth could not walk with me in her arms without feeling Viv's eyes watching her.

The torment became too much. Ruth's nights were full of fear. Each morning, she woke up waiting for the next attack. Viv's threats grew darker. She said she would not stop until Ruth was gone. Fear finally took hold of Ruth's heart. She knew she could not fight a woman so set on hurting her.

Before leaving the city, Ruth tried to hold on to the one thing she loved most. She begged to keep me with her. She asked for custody, but Robert refused. People believed his word more, and he won.

It happened after a talk he had with Viv the night before.

He sat in her small sitting room. The lamps gave off a weak light, and long shadows covered the walls. Viv poured him a glass of rum and leaned close. Her voice was soft and calm.

"So, she is leaving," Viv said, her eyes fixed on him. "Running away, just like I said. And she plans to take your child with her."

Robert stared into his drink. His jaw was tight. "She says she wants a new start," he muttered. "She thinks it will be better for the baby."

Viv gave a soft laugh, bitter and mocking. "Better for the baby, or better for her? Do you not see it? She does not care about you, Robert. She was ready to walk away and take what belongs to you. That is not love. That is betrayal."

He shifted in his chair, uneasy. "She is still the mother of my daughter."

Viv's eyes sharpened, though her lips curved into a smile. "A mother who would have stolen her from you. You should be glad she is leaving. Let her go. Let her carry her troubles elsewhere. Why tie yourself to a woman who was already ready to cut you out of her life?"

Robert looked at her sternly. "I will not part with my daughter."

He said that because he still loved me, the daughter who resembled him, no matter how deceitful he was being.

A flicker of disgust crossed Viv's face, gone as quickly as it appeared. The thought of raising Ruth's child made her blood burn, but she smoothed her expression and let her voice drip with sweetness.

"If that is what you need, then keep her," she said softly. "Let Ruth fend for herself in whatever country she runs to. You and I will build our life here, Robert. With or without her."

He looked at her, torn, but her words dug deep into his heart. Slowly, he nodded, surrendering to the choice she had laid before him.

Viv leaned back, her smile faint but satisfied. Ruth might escape, but she would not escape without loss.

***

The fight for custody ended against my mother. The decision broke her heart. She went back to her hometown with tears in her eyes and no strength left in her body. Every step she took away from me was heavy with pain that no one could comfort.

After Robert took me and moved in with Viv, everything grew sad. Viv did not want me there. She had Robert now, but she could not forget Ruth. Another woman had a child for him, almost the same age as me, and that thought never stopped hurting her.

Still, Viv was brilliant. She knew that if she wanted to stay in Robert's life, she had to look kind and gentle. So she acted like a loving stepmother. She smiled when Robert looked her way. She pretended to be patient, even when she was not.

But inside, her anger deepened. Each time she saw me, she saw Ruth, even though I looked like my father, and her hatred grew stronger. It did not matter that Viv had been the one to break their family. What ruled her heart was jealousy and pride. She wanted to erase every part of Ruth's memory.

When I turned one, my mother was still broken, but my father stood in a church beside Viv. The bells rang. People cheered. He smiled as if nothing had been lost. They were married. Viv became Mrs. Hanson, just like she had wanted. Their vows sounded as if the past had never existed.

For my mother, her world was gone. For me, too small to understand, it was the beginning of a new life. The story of Ruth and Robert had ended. But mine had just begun—with Viv no longer just a neighbor, but the shadow that would follow me everywhere.

Chapter 3: The Countryside

Life under Viv and my father was nothing like the home I had been born into.

Viv, who became pregnant soon after their marriage, hated me with a fire I could never escape. Her hatred was not quiet or hidden. It lived in her eyes each time she looked at me. It was because I kept reminding her of Ruth—the woman Viv despised more than anyone. Every line in my face, every trace of my mother that showed itself in me, was enough to turn Viv's heart colder.

My father did not hate me. It seemed like he did—by the way he had abandoned my mother, but that was never true. He loved me in his own quiet way, though he didn't show it physically. I could see it in his eyes when he thought no one was watching.

He saw how Viv treated me, but he did not stop her. Instead, he stayed silent. He worked late, came home tired, and let Viv decide how things should be. She had a way of bending his will, and he followed her more than he should have.

When he was home, he kept his distance. I was there, yet it felt like he was far away. He sometimes spoke softly to me, as if afraid that Viv might hear. It was easier for him to stay quiet than to start a fight he could not win.

He loved me, I know he did. But his love lived in silence, trapped under Viv's shadow. And because of that, the bond between us grew thin, stretched by fear and things left unsaid.

Viv's own child grew in her belly, and that only made her cruelty much worse. She would sit in her chair, her hand resting on her stomach, and stare at me with a scowl.

"You should be grateful you have a roof over your head," she muttered once when I walked too close, although I was just a baby. I froze, unsure if she was speaking to me, but her glare told me she was.

In fact, her cruelty knew no bounds.

She did not smile at me anymore. Sometimes she took my food away or pushed my hand when I reached for something. I did not understand why. The house felt cold, even when the lamps were bright. I learned to be quiet, to stay small.

One night, loud voices woke me. They came from the sitting room. Viv was shouting. Her voice was sharp, like glass breaking. My father's voice was low and tired.

"Viv, stop this," he said. "She's just a little girl."

Viv's voice grew louder. "A little girl? She's *Ruth's* child!" she yelled. "Do you think I can forget that?"

I was standing by the door, holding my blanket. My chest hurt from fear. My father saw me and said softly, "Elaina, everything is okay."

But before I could move, Viv came toward me. Her eyes looked wild. "Don't look at me like that!" she shouted. Her hand grabbed my chest. It hurt so much that I screamed. My father ran to us and pulled her away.

"Viv, enough!" he shouted. His voice sounded angry and broken.

I sat on the floor crying. My chest burned where her hand had been. My father knelt beside me, his hands shaking. "Elaina," he whispered, but Viv was still shouting, and he turned away.

Later that night, the house was quiet. My father came to my room. I was lying in bed, holding my doll. He sat beside me and touched my hair. His hand was soft, but I could feel the sadness in it.

"I'm sorry," he said in a small voice. I didn't know what the words meant, but his face looked like he wanted to cry. He kissed my forehead, then left the room.

After that night, Viv did not shout as much. She smiled when Father was home, but her eyes turned cold again when he left. I was too little to understand her words, but I knew she did not want me there.

***

One hot afternoon, when I was some months over a year old, just shy of two years, Viv's patience with me finally snapped. She was heavily pregnant, her belly huge, fanning herself on the veranda, her face distorted with irritation. I toddled across the floor, reaching for a wooden spoon that had fallen from the table. My laughter rose in the air, and it made Viv's scowl even more pronounced.

"She is always underfoot," Viv said sharply to my father, who sat nearby reading the newspaper. "I am about to have a baby of my own. I cannot keep raising that child while I am carrying another."

My father lowered the paper, his brow furrowed. "She is just a baby, Viv. What do you expect me to do?"

Viv's voice softened, though her words cut just as deep. "Send her to my people in the country. My mother will take her in. She will be fed, cared for, and kept out of the way there. You know I am right. Look at me." She gestured at her swollen belly. "I cannot have her here, disturbing me day and night."

He said nothing at first, staring at the paper as if searching for an answer in the print. I reached up toward him, and he looked at me. His eyes were troubled. Viv pressed on, her tone sweet, convincing, the way she always spoke when she wanted her way.

"You would be doing her a favor. Family, fresh air, and open fields would surround her. It will be better for her. Don't you see?"

At last, he folded the paper and nodded. "Perhaps you are right. Perhaps it is for the best."

And just like that, a choice was made.

My life was pushed aside with a nod, and I was packed for the country.

***

The path to take was a long, windy one. My father took me on the bus, and he held me tight against his chest. His arms were stiff, like I might fly away if he loosened his hold.

The journey to the country went whizzing past me in half-formed shapes and colors, but I recall the feel of his arms as he took me up the narrow road to the old farmhouse. I held on to his collar, my face against his shoulder, as I watched the sky above change its shade as dusk approached. He stared straight on, his jaws clenched, as though even this walk weighed down on him.

He knocked on the front door of the old house in a field. An elderly woman answered it.

Viv's mother.

Her eyes flicked over Robert first, then me, and her mouth pressed into a thin line. She did not reach for me right away. Instead, she wiped her hands on her apron and stepped back to let us in.

Her eyes studied Robert first before shifting to me. I matched her gaze with a starry-eyed one, and she pressed her lips into a thin line. She wiped her hands on her apron and stepped aside to let my father in.

"Evening," Robert said, voice flat. "She's yours for a while."

The older woman gave a short nod. "So, I heard."

She didn't look at me when she said it. Later, I would learn why, because a letter had arrived days before, written in Viv's sharp hand. In it, she explained that she was carrying Robert's child now, their *real* child, and she did not have the strength or the desire to care for the shadow of Ruth. That was how she described me: *the shadow of Ruth.* Her mother had read every word, folded the letter neatly, and put it in a drawer. From that moment on, her duty was clear. Not warmth, not affection. Only responsibility.

Inside the house, a teenager came forward, her eyes curious. She bent down and brushed her finger against my cheek. "She's a quiet one," she said. "Does she talk yet?"

"She's barely a year old," Robert muttered. He shifted me in his arms. "Doesn't say much. Just… cries, sometimes."

The girl chuckled, leaning closer to tickle my chin. "She's sweet. Can I hold her?"

Before Robert could answer, Viv's mother reached out and took me. Her grip felt firm but not tender. She studied me for a moment, her gaze lingering on the shape of my eyes and the line of my mouth. I smiled up at her and reached for her necklace. She did not smile back.

"We'll manage," she said. "Put her things in the back room."

Robert hesitated, shifting from one foot to the other. His hands trembled as he tried to speak. "I'll come by when I can," he said, his voice low. It was an empty promise because Viv wouldn't let him.

He looked at me then, and for a moment, the mask he wore every day slipped away. His eyes were full of sorrow –the kind that comes from love mixed with guilt. He wanted to reach for me, but he didn't. His lips parted, as if he wanted to say something more, something that might make it easier, but no words came.

When he finally turned to go, his shoulders sagged. Each step he took away from me looked heavy, as though his heart was fighting his body. His footsteps faded down the path, slow and uneven, until all I could hear were the crickets in the grass and my quiet breathing.

He hadn't left because he stopped loving me. He left because he didn't know how to fight for me.

That evening, they gave me a small piece of sweet bread to hold. Sugar stuck to my fingers, and I laughed when the teenager helped me lick it off. For a moment, I felt lightness. They spread a cloth on the floor and laid me there. My small body rested inside the chatter of strangers. A lantern glowed on the table, and shadows moved across the walls.

"She'll be no trouble," the girl whispered, watching me yawn.

"She'll be working," her mother corrected, adjusting her apron. Her voice carried no malice, only weariness. "Don't confuse the two."

I was too small to understand her words. My eyes drooped, my fists opened, and I drifted into the first peaceful sleep I would ever know in that house.

Peace lasted only a short time. I did not know it then as I lay on that cloth with the cool night air brushing over me, but the sweetness of that day would not last. The letter had already poisoned the soil beneath me. They did not see me as a child to love but as a burden to bear. As I grew, that truth pressed itself deeper into my life.

Sleep closed over me, and my heart surrendered to the unknowing dreams of a child who had not yet learned what suffering was.

I had no idea of the kind of Hell I was going to be put through here.

***

By the time I turned two, the warmth of that first day was gone. What little kindness there had been slowly slipped away until there was nothing left. I wandered the house alone, small feet padding across cold floors, reaching for hands that rarely reached back. My cries echoed in corners, unanswered, swallowed by walls that had grown used to ignoring me.

Viv's mother was the hardest of them all. She did not hide her disdain when she looked at me. Her eyes narrowed as though every feature on my face reminded her of Ruth, the woman Viv had painted as an enemy. She gave me food, but not affection. She clothed me, but not gently. To her, I was a task, nothing more.

The teenager, who once smiled and played, grew distracted. She had her own world to chase and dreams to think about. Sometimes she watched me with a look of guilt, as though she knew I needed more, but she never acted. When I reached for her hand, she often pulled it away, too busy to bother.

I spent long days in silence, sitting by the window or crawling after scraps of attention. My small voice filled the air with cries no one cared to soothe. I was too little to understand why the world around me had turned cold. All I knew was the ache of being unseen.

The house itself began to feel larger, emptier. Meals passed without anyone speaking to me. Nights stretched long with nothing but the sound of my own sobs in the dark. Sometimes I fell asleep with wet cheeks, still whimpering for someone who never came.

At that age, I did not have words for cruelty. I only knew the sharp sting of being unwanted. The woman who should have been a grandmother looked through me as if I were invisible. And I was. I lived in her house, ate her food, breathed her air, but I did not live in her heart.

When I turned four, the indifference around me sharpened into something harsher. I was no longer just ignored. I was given tasks, chores meant for hands larger than mine. Viv's mother decided I was old enough to be useful. To her, I was not a child who needed care but an extra pair of hands to lighten her own work.

Each morning, she would hand me a small cloth and order me to wipe the floors. My tiny arms dragged the cloth back and forth, leaving streaks across the wooden boards. If I missed a spot, she would click her tongue and mutter about my mother, as though Ruth herself had failed through me.

"Do it again," she would say, snatching the cloth from me and shoving it back into my hands. "You are no good unless you learn to work, nor will you grow strong by sitting idle.

I watched other children my age in the village chase each other in play, their laughter ringing through the fields. My laughter was replaced by scrubbing, fetching, and carrying. The teenager who once smiled at me no longer intervened. She had grown older, and like her mother, saw me as nothing more than a responsibility. If I cried too much, she scolded me. If I lagged, she sighed in frustration.

Nights were the worst. My small body ached from bending and lifting. My fingers stung from rough cloths and splinters. I curled up on my bed, trying to remember if anyone had ever truly held me close. My memories of Ruth were already faint, but I clung to them, reaching for warmth that lived only in fragments of dreams.

By four, I should have been playing with dolls, singing little songs, and learning words of kindness. Instead, I was taught how to obey, how to silence my cries, and how to survive in a house that never wanted me.

***

That evening, the smell of stew filled the house. My stomach twisted as I watched the pot bubbling on the stove. The sound of spoons clinking against bowls was like a drumbeat in my ears. I sat quietly in the corner, waiting, hoping they might remember I was hungry too this time.

Viv's mother ladled stew into bowls, one for herself, one for the teenager, one for Robert when he came. When she reached the bottom of the pot, she scraped what was left into her own dish, not even glancing my way.

I whispered, "May I have some, please?" My voice came out so small I barely heard it myself.

Her head snapped toward me. "You had bread this morning. That is enough for a girl like you."

The teenager looked at me for a moment, her spoon frozen halfway to her mouth. Our eyes met. There was a breath of expectation, as if she would reply. She bent her head and began to eat, her silence speaking more than words.

My hands shook in my lap. I held them together to stop myself from crying, but tears came anyway, hot and fast. "I am hungry," I said, louder this time, though my words trembled.

The woman slammed her spoon against the table. "Ungrateful child! You will learn to keep quiet." Her voice cracked through the room like a whip.

Silence filled the space. Only the scrape of spoons against bowls and the soft chewing of food I could not taste broke it. My belly ached so badly it felt like fire inside me. I stared at the floor, counting the lines in the wood, trying not to sob.

When they finished, they ordered me to wash the dishes. My arms felt weak and my legs shaky, but I obeyed. The smell of food clung to the bowls, making my hunger even stronger with every plate I rinsed.

Later, when the house grew dark, I lay in bed with nothing in my stomach. My eyes stayed open, wide and wet. Hunger moved through my body until I was too tired to cry anymore.

That night, I understood something I had not before. This was not forgetfulness. This was not a mistake. It was chosen, deliberate. They wanted me small, voiceless, and broken.

This treatment continued day after day. Hunger turned into a shadow that followed me everywhere. I grew thin and weak, my arms and legs like sticks, my clothes hanging loose. Their harsh words stung as much as my empty stomach. I could not understand why they treated me this way. I was still only a child, too small to know what I had done wrong. At night, I lay awake staring at the dark ceiling, wondering how long this cruelty would last. I wondered if there would ever be a day when someone would come for me, hold me, feed me, and tell me I mattered.

Chapter 4: My Saving Grace

The days in that house never seemed to end. Every morning, my stomach hurt, the hunger gnawing at me like a monster. Every night I went to sleep, the pain made me wheeze. I was only four years old. But I already understood. Understood what it felt like when nobody wanted you. No one was kind to me at all. No one ever smiled at me. They told me to be quiet. To make myself small. To never ask for food.

I sat by myself on the cold floor. Thinking about the woman Viv called Ruth. She was my real mother. Viv always said her name as if it were something dirty. Like a word you shouldn't say out loud. She told me Ruth ran away. She left me here. I was too little to remember what actually happened. I couldn't figure out why she didn't want me now.

Sometimes I tried to picture her face. I imagined someone with my own face. Someone who would scoop me up. Who would hold me tight. When I thought about her for too long, something in my chest started aching badly. My eyes would fill up with tears. I kept thinking: *if she had only stayed. Maybe things would be different now. Maybe I would have food to eat. Maybe someone would love me finally.*

When nighttime came, and the house got quiet, I would whisper to her. Whisper in the darkness. I asked her why she left me alone. I asked her if she ever thought about me at all. I cried so much that my pillow got soaking wet. I told her I hated her for going away. I hated her for not picking me.

The things Viv said cut deep inside me. She kept saying Ruth left because she didn't want me. After hearing it enough times, I started believing it must be the truth. Maybe I really was a mistake. Everyone in that house treated me like I was a mistake. Viv treated me that way. Even her family, who tossed me bits of food like I was a dog, and told me I should be grateful for it.

Everything felt too big around me. And I felt too small always. I just wanted to vanish completely. I wanted my stomach to stop hurting all the time. I wanted all the sad feelings to go away forever. I wanted to stop feeling bad about being born. I didn't understand much about anything else. But I understood this one thing clearly:

If my mother really loved me at all, she would have come back for me.

She never came back. So, I figured nobody ever would.

***

While I was lost in my own sadness, something else happened back home.

Rose was my grandmother and Robert's mother. She moved with quiet grace. Her presence was gentle but strong, like a soft breeze that lingers. She was the only person in that house who truly cared for me. I didn't understand it then. Her care showed in small ways. Simple questions. Small acts that seemed normal.

She knew what I didn't. She knew Viv hated me. The signs were clear to her. Viv's words were sharp. Even when she smiled, her eyes showed anger. Whenever I entered a room, or when she had to touch me at all, her hands would shake.

Rose saw it all clearly. But she couldn't stop it.

All she could do was watch quietly. Her kind eyes followed me always, like a guardian who couldn't step in to help.

"Are you eating enough, dear?" she would ask in her soft voice. Her hands were working on the yarn as she knitted a sweater.

"Yes, Grandma," I would answer back. Not knowing why, she asked that question constantly.

She would nod slowly. Then glance at Viv. Viv was always nearby, pretending to smile for her.

"Oh yes," Viv would say with fake cheer. "She's eating fine. Just being a little troublemaker, as always!"

Rose would nod again. But the worry never left her kind face. For a while, she believed Viv's words. Maybe she wanted to believe them. Because it was easier than facing the hard truth, but when Viv turned away, Rose would look at me. Her eyes spoke what she could not say out loud.

They said: *I see you. I know what they do to you. I am here for you, even if I cannot help you now.*

As a child, that was enough for me entirely. I didn't understand the words. But I felt her deep warmth—warmth which was quiet and gentle. In a house with fake smiles, hers felt like home to me.

When I was sent away, Rose's worry turned to deep fear. The thought of sending a small child, only two years old, to live with strangers broke her heart completely. She had always tried to respect the boundaries set. But this was too far now. It made her chest tighten hard. It made her hands shake.

One afternoon, she finally spoke up about it. Her voice trembled with anger and pain.

"Robert, why are you sending her away?" she asked him. She held the edge of the kitchen table for strength. "She's only two years old! She doesn't understand any of this. She shouldn't have to go through that kind of pain."

Robert sighed heavily. His shoulders sagged.

"Viv says she should leave. She can't take care of two children at once. The new baby is coming soon."

Rose's heart sank completely. She had seen that fake kindness in Viv's eyes too many times to be fooled. This wasn't about the new baby coming. Viv wanted me gone. Out of her sight. Forgotten forever.

"You're saying it's for her own good?" Rose said, her voice shaking badly. "Sending her away to complete strangers? At this age? Don't you see what that will do to her inside?"

Robert didn't answer her at all. His silence said everything clearly.

Rose's worry only grew heavier. She paced quietly in her small sitting room, hands clasped together, muttering under her breath. Every shadow felt darker now, and every laugh that wasn't mine seemed sharper to her. Her mind raced with plans, wondering how she could protect me, especially from the people who were supposed to care the most.

The whole time I was away, Rose never stopped asking about me. She would constantly ask Viv and Robert about me. Her concern was woven into every question. Gentle, but persistent.

"Elaina," she would ask softly, "how is she doing there now? Is she eating well? Is she happy there? Are they treating her kindly at all?"

Viv always flashed that strained, forced smile. Tilting her head just so. "Yes, yes, don't worry, Rose," she would say. Her voice was too bright. Too rehearsed now. "My folks are taking care of her well enough. She's happier there than she was here, truly."

But this time, Rose did not believe a single word. Her eyes, sharp despite their age, betrayed her deep disbelief. She knew Viv too well. Knew the quiet bitterness she held for my mother. Knew how that hatred colored every decision. Viv couldn't have sent me to a place where I was treated like a princess. She must have left instructions that I was not to be pampered. Not to be loved. Nor to be cared.

Rose's heart ached with worry. A gnawing, constant ache that would not fade away. Every unanswered letter. Every too-bright smile from Viv – it all confirmed her deep suspicion. I was not being treated as I should have been treated.

She sat quietly in her armchair, knitting needles idly tapping as her eyes stared into the distance. "My poor little Elaina," she whispered one evening, her voice trembling. "I hope she knows… I hope she feels… that I am with her, even if only in my heart."

One afternoon, while I was wallowing in my room back at the farm, Rose spoke to her son with a determination that was rare for her. Her voice was gentle, but it carried a hard edge of resolve.

"I'm going to visit Elaina," she said clearly, looking Robert directly in his eyes. "I need to see how she's doing for myself now."

At first, Robert's heart leaped. The idea of finally knowing how I was, of seeing me again, thrilled and terrified him. But he knew better than to act on impulse. Viv had made it very clear: he was never to visit me.

She repeated it constantly, her voice sharp. "She's with her relatives now. Let her be and do not look back."

Robert obeyed her, but he stayed in contact through letters. Letters Viv always claimed were sent to me, even though it was a blatant lie, since I never replied.

Hearing his mother's plan, his heart raced hard. He almost blurted out that he wanted to go with her, to see me too, but he thought better of it fast. His daughter with Viv was almost three now, and he knew mentioning a visit would send Viv into a furious rage. So, he swallowed his longing whole and simply nodded slowly, forcing calm onto his face.

"Okay, Mother," he said quietly. "Do what you must do."

Rose reached across the table. She placed her hand on his arm gently. "Robert," she said softly, "you must promise me something now. Don't tell Viv I'm going. She must not know this."

He met her gaze steadily, feeling the weight of her words. The truth behind them was heavy.

"I promise," he said. He meant it deeply. He was hoping with all his heart. Hoping I was safe. Hoping I was okay. That this visit would reassure them. That I was still a little girl. A girl who deserved love and care.

***

Soon, the day arrived. Rose set off, taking the same train and following the same winding path Robert had taken almost three years ago. When he dropped me off at that farm, the rhythmic clatter of the train had felt comforting at first, but as the landscape changed and familiar fields came into view, a tight knot formed in her chest.

Her heart grew heavier with every mile. Something deep inside told her something was wrong. Something more than simple motherly worry. A cold, unshakable premonition whispered loudly that what awaited her might be far worse than she was anticipating.

Worse than she could ever imagine.

When she reached the farm, the air was thick with the scent of earth and hay. The quiet hum of life deepened her unease. Taking a steadying breath, she walked up to the front door. She knocked on it, her knuckles brushing the worn wood.

The door opened now. A young woman stood there. The daughter of the family caring for me—that teenager. Her expression was neutral. Rose introduced herself calmly. However, her chest tightened with urgency inside.

"I'm Elaina's grandmother," she said. "May I see her, please?"

The girl simply nodded. Without a word, she stepped aside. She led Rose quietly through the house, the wood floor creaking beneath their feet. She guided her toward the back. A small, modest room waited there. She opened the door and gestured for her to enter.

"This is her room," she said softly. Then, without another word, she left, leaving Rose to enter the room on her own.

Rose paused in the doorway, taking in the small, tidy room. Her heart was pounding hard now. Everything looked too orderly, as if the arrangement hid something deeper inside. And then she called my name. Her voice was trembling slightly, but filled with a grandmother's determination.

"Elaina... It's Grandma. Are you here, my dear?"

Inside, the room was dim. The light from the small window barely reached the far corner—the corner where I sat huddled.

And then Rose saw me. A cold, unbearable shock swept over her entire body. Her mouth dropped open wide. For a moment, she couldn't breathe at all.

I was huddled there tightly, as small and fragile as a bird with broken wings. My arms were wrapped tight around my knees. My tiny frame seemed impossibly thin, like I was only skin stretched over bones now. The long periods of neglect and starvation had carved their mark on my body, leaving me frail, fragile, and completely exhausted.

Rose's heart constricted painfully. She took a tentative step slowly inside the room. Every instinct screamed at her, urging her to gather me up, shield me from this world, and somehow make everything right again. But I didn't have the strength to lift my head, let alone look at her. My dark eyes stayed fixed on the floor; my small body curled inward. As if trying to make myself totally invisible.

"Elaina, dear?"

The voice was soft, uncertain, and trembling badly.

I looked up slowly now. My movements were sluggish and heavy. It was as though even lifting my head took all the strength I had left inside. The woman standing in the doorway was a stranger to me. Her eyes were wide with disbelief, her hand pressed hard to her chest. I didn't recognize her at all. I had been barely two when I was sent away. I don't remember ever having a grandmother.

Rose's eyes filled with tears instantly. The moment our gazes met. She took a step closer now. Her breath caught in her throat as she took in the sight of me, my thin arms, and my hollow cheeks. My clothes hung off my tiny frame, like they belonged to someone else entirely.

"Oh, my poor child..." she whispered low, her voice cracking now. She knelt right beside me and clasped her trembling hands together tightly. "God, please watch over this little one," she murmured under her breath, barely holding herself together now. Then, with a sudden spark of determination, she whispered fiercely, "I'm telling your father to come and get you right now, to take you away from these monsters."

Her words drifted toward me, soft and distant, as if they were carried through water. I heard them vaguely, but I couldn't truly understand them. My body was too weak. My mind was too tired now. Hunger had long ago dulled my thoughts. I didn't even have the energy to wonder who she was. So, I simply lay my head back on my knees and stayed completely still.

Rose's heart broke. She watched me sink into silence. Her hands shook as she fumbled with her purse, rummaging desperately until she found a small bun from her journey. She unwrapped it carefully, holding it out to me.

"Here, sweetheart," she said gently. "Eat, please."

I took it with trembling fingers. The bread was dry. Crumbling at the edges. But I ate it slowly, piece by tiny piece, like it was dust, not food. My lips barely moved now. My eyes were dull and far away.

Rose pressed her hand to her mouth, stifling a sob. Tears slipped down her cheeks. She watched her granddaughter, her son's child, devour a scrap of bread like it was a feast.

"Oh, Elaina..." she whispered with a tight throat. "What have they done to you?"

In that small, dark room, Rose made a silent vow. She would not leave me there. She would not rest until I was completely free, whatever it took, whatever battle she had to fight. She would be my saving grace. She would tear me away from this cruelty, from these people who had turned my innocence into suffering.

Rose went back home the very next morning. She didn't rest, didn't stop to eat, didn't even change her clothes. The whole train ride back, her mind raced, filled with the image of me, small, frail, lifeless. By the time she reached town, her hands were shaking, and her face was pale with exhaustion and fury.

She went straight to Robert's house. When he opened the door, the look on her face stopped him cold.

"Mother? What's wrong?" he asked her. His voice was uneasy.

Rose didn't answer right away. Her eyes brimmed with tears. She stepped inside. She clutched his arm tight.

"Robert," she said, her voice breaking. "You have to bring Elaina back home now."

He frowned, confused and frightened by her. "Bring her back? What do you mean? I thought she was doing fine. Viv said—"

"Viv lied!" Rose snapped. Her voice trembled with anger now. "She's starving, Robert! That child, your daughter, is wasting away to nothing. They've been starving her on purpose! I saw her with my own eyes. Skin and bones. Sitting alone in that dark room. She didn't even recognize me."

Robert's heart sank like a stone in water. He staggered back a step, pressing a hand to his forehead as if the words were too heavy to bear.

"No..." he whispered low, shaking his head constantly. "No, that can't be true."

Rose's tears spilled over then. "If you don't bring her home, she will die there," she cried out. "Do you understand that? They're killing her slowly. You cannot leave her another day in that terrible place."

Robert stood still. His face was pale, his breath shallow. A father's guilt pressed against his chest, squeezing him until he could barely speak a word. For a long moment, the room was silent except for Rose's quiet sobs.

Then, without another word, he turned. He walked toward the small desk by the window, grabbed his coat, and reached for his keys.

"I'll go," he said simply. His voice was low, steady, and trembling with remorse now. "I'm going to get her myself."

Robert's worst mistake, which he realized too late, was telling Viv his plan.

As the words left his mouth, she erupted. Viv's face twisted with fury. Her voice was sharp and high-pitched, cutting through the house like a whip.

"You're not bringing her back!" she shrieked, pacing now. Her hands were trembling with rage. "Jezzy is already here! You can't just add more burden to us!"

Robert stood his ground. His jaw was tight, and his heart was pounding. His calm words were useless now. Her fury was a storm, but he wouldn't let it sway him this time.

"This isn't about Jezzy," he said firmly, "It's about Elaina. She's suffering. She's being starved, and I will not leave her there to die."

Viv threw her hands up, her eyes blazing. "How dare you! You're choosing her over our child! Over me!"

Robert said nothing more. He turned on his heel, grabbed his coat and his bag. Every step felt like breaking an invisible chain, but he knew there was no turning back for him.

"I'm leaving," he said simply. His voice was steady now. "And I'm not listening to another word you say."

Viv's scream followed him down the stairs, but Robert didn't falter. He walked out through the familiar streets toward the train station, the train that would take him back to Elaina, back to the daughter he had failed but now had the chance to save.

The train ride felt endless to Robert. Each clatter of the wheels echoed his pounding heart. He replayed the image of Elaina huddled in that corner, frail, tiny, hollow-eyed. Every mile drew him closer but also deeper into the years of guilt he carried.

When he finally arrived at the farm, his steps were hurried and uneven. The air smelled of damp earth, but he hardly noticed it. His focus was only on finding her, seeing her alive.

The front door opened, and the same young woman appeared. She nodded silently, leading him to the back of the house, to the small, dim room, my prison.

And there I was.

The moment I saw him, recognition sparked in my eyes. "Daddy!" I cried out. My small arms flinging open. I stumbled toward him. My voice was weak. Cracked. Desperate.

Robert froze for a heartbeat, stunned completely. I ran into his embrace. The sight of my tiny, frail body nearly broke him. I clung to him, sobbing. My head was buried in his chest. "Daddy… I… I'm hungry… I'm… tired…"

Robert's chest tightened hard. Every step he had taken to leave me. Every excuse he had made. Every moment, he had believed Viv's lies. It all crashed down on him at once. "Oh, Elaina… my sweet girl," he whispered. His voice was thick with tears. "I'm so, so sorry. I should have never left you here at all."

He lifted me carefully into his arms, cradling my fragile body, as if holding me too tightly might shatter me completely. My petite frame felt like a feather, yet every ounce of my suffering weighed on him like a ton of unshakeable guilt.

When they finally arrived at the house, Rose was waiting, tears streaming down her face. She reached out immediately, wrapping me in her arms as Robert placed me down. "You're home, Elaina," Rose whispered, kissing my forehead gently. "You're safe now. Safe at last."

But that couldn't be further from the truth.

Chapter 5:
The Fate of Elaina

The first thing I noticed when I returned home was the smell of food. My grandmother was working in the kitchen for me and her granddaughter, baking bread and cooking stew. The smell infiltrated my nose like a greeting.

But even warmth can sting when it has been gone for too long.

My grandmother, Rose, fussed over me that first night, setting out a bowl of delicious meaty stew and two slices of buttered bread. The richness of it made me dizzy. My hands trembled as I held the spoon, half-afraid it would be taken away again.

Robert sat across the table, silent, his eyes on his plate.

Viv was not there.

For the first few days, things almost seemed *better*. Grandma made sure I had proper meals, clean clothes, and a warm bath each night. She even brushed my hair the way mothers were supposed to. But beneath that kindness, a shadow lurked and had a name.

Viv.

When Viv returned from her friend's house, her smile was stretched too wide. She kissed Rose on both cheeks, thanked Robert for "keeping things in order," and then turned to me with eyes like cold mirrors.

"My, you look well-fed," she said, her voice dripping honey. "We must make sure you don't lose your…figure."

From that day, much to my dismay, things returned to how they were before I was sent away. This time, though, they were worse.

Because Viv was absolutely furious that I was back.

Meals were no longer denied but came with words sharper than hunger. Every bite tasted of humiliation—little comments, mocking tones, the constant reminder that kindness came at Viv's mercy.

Viv would stand behind me at the dinner table, fingers resting lightly on my shoulders.

"Eat," she'd whisper. "You wouldn't want to make Grandma think I starve you again, now would you?"

And then there was Jezzy.

Jezzy, the name Viv had given to her own daughter, was the center of attention in the household. As we girls grew up, and Ryan, Jezzy's brother and my half-brother, was introduced in the picture, things only went from bad to worse for me. I was constantly compared with my half-sister by Viv's punitive tongue, although I was two years older.

"Elaina, see how Jezzy sits so straight?"

"Elaina, why can't you play the piano as sweetly as Jezzy?"

"Elaina, don't frown – you'll frighten Jezzy."

My father noticed…sometimes. His mouth would twitch, as if he wanted to say something but thought better of it, and let the words die in his throat. Grandma noticed, too, but unlike her son, she *did* speak. Quietly, gently, her words rolled off Viv like rain on glass.

"Let the girl be, Viv," she'd say. "She's been through enough."

Viv would only smile. “I’m teaching her discipline, Mother. You wouldn’t want her growing up spoiled.”

I would lie awake at night, staring at the ceiling and its cracked plaster. It reminded me of myself—a thousand thin lines holding back the collapse.

I wasn’t starving anymore. But sometimes, I wished I were. Hunger, at least, was simple. It didn’t whisper lies. It didn’t laugh at me when I cried.

Despite everything, somewhere deep inside, a stubborn ember refused to die. Maybe it was Rose’s touch that soothed my distraught nerves. Maybe my father’s silence was laden with guilt so hefty that I could feel it. Or perhaps it was something inside me, something even Viv couldn’t stamp out.

Whatever it was, it whispered to me when the house went dark:

You’re still here. You’re still you. Don’t let them take that, too.

***

Years slipped by like dust caught in sunlight, beautiful from a distance, choking up close.

I grew, though no one seemed to notice.

I was eight now. I was a small girl, tranquil, with eyes that nervously kept darting here and there… eyes that once held light but had now grown dim. My hands were always busy: scrubbing, polishing, mending. They’d grown rough for a child’s, small maps of all the work I was never thanked for.

Jezzy, two years younger, was everything Viv hoped her to be—pretty, loud, and with no care in the world. Her friends came around on weekends, and their laughter could be heard all along the halls like music in a different world.

Three years younger than me, Ryan was the golden child—smart, mischievous, and already following his father in charisma. However, the kindness in him was usually choked by the poison that pervaded the homestead.

And me? I was the ghost that kept the house breathing.

My father, Robert, rarely came home before dusk anymore. When he did, Viv made sure his evenings were wrapped in comfort and flattery. She spoke softly, smiled just enough, and filled his ears with tales of my "fragile nerves" and "bad attitude."

"She doesn't belong out there, Robert," Viv would sigh, setting down his dinner plate with the grace of a saint. "You know what people will say. Best she stay home until she learns her place."

And my father, worn down and weary, would nod, too tired to question, too guilty to see.

Grandma tried, for as long as she could. She'd stand by the window some mornings, watching me sweep the front steps while the neighbor's children passed by on their way to school.

"Let her go, Viv," Rose would whisper. "She's got a good mind. You can't keep her here forever."

Viv would only smile. That same smile, thin and sharp, as if she were only looking out for my best interests.

"Forever's a long time, Mother. I'm not keeping her forever. Just until she's *useful.*"

And so, I stayed.

The days lapsed into each other: morning, evening, night. I saw Jezzy and Ryan swell and thrive under their mother's eyes while I faded in the background. When they walked away—to school, parties, and places I would never see—I would be at the window, and see myself in the mirror before the glass reclaimed me.

At times, when I saw my own reflection in a mirror, I could hardly recognize myself. The girl who once played till her arms grew tired, who thought stars in the sky were huge blinking eyes, was reduced to nothing but a weak mess, made only for house chores and snapping words.

However, something in me still flickered. Viv noticed it, too, and she tried to blow it out.

"Elaina," she'd call sweetly, "the floors need scrubbing again. You missed a spot yesterday." Or, "Don't slouch. No wonder no one looks at you twice."

Or, worse—silence. That pointed, deliberate silence that said: *You don't exist here unless I decide you do.*

And my father?

He saw, sometimes. In the way I flinched when Viv entered the room, in how my voice barely rose above a whisper. But by the time he opened his mouth to speak, Viv's hand was already on his arm, her voice a soft murmur:

"She's fine, Robert. You worry too much. You know how sensitive she is."

Just like that, the truth would slip away again.

So, I worked. I washed the linens, polished the silver, tended the garden I could never enjoy. My world was small—four walls, a cruel face instead of a loving mother, and memories of what freedom used to taste like.

However, at times, when the wind was passing through the open window and bringing laughter from the street beyond, I would stop. Just for a heartbeat, I would shut my eyes and daydream about going outside, seeing the sun come upon my cheeks, and my name being called with kindness, affection, and fondness.

And in that small, stubborn imagining, something still lived.

Not hope. At least not yet.

But the faint, trembling outline of it.

***

As I grew up, Viv's cruelty knew no bounds. It showed up in different ways and methods, each worse than the last.

One day, morning light was creeping through the kitchen window, warming up my hands as I carefully stirred the pot of porridge on the stove, my senses on alert because Viv was watching from the back.

"Don't let it burn, girl," she warned, her voice both sickly sweet and dangerous.

I nodded quickly. "Yes, ma'am."

The porridge kept cooking on, its surface creating bubbles. I kept stirring it, making sure to keep my focus sharp. However, misfortune hit both me and the porridge, as the fire under the stove suddenly raged, causing the entire dish to burn.

My heart jumped into my mouth. And for good reason, because Viv had gotten up.

"Useless child!"

The wooden spoon was snatched from my hand and smacked across my knuckles, causing a wave of pain to run through my entire arm. I bit my lip to stop the tears from falling down my cheeks.

"Do you know how much food you waste?" Viv hissed, her face inches from the mine. "Maybe I should feed you what you ruin. Would you like that?"

I shook my head, silent.

"Then eat it anyway."

And I did—sitting at the kitchen corner, choking down bitter, scorched porridge while Viv hummed a tune and served Jezzy and Ryan from a fresh pot.

***

Another time, it was Jezzy's 6th birthday. The parlor was filled with flowers, ribbons, and laughter, and my job was to ensure no speck of dust touched the floor.

"Mama, can Elaina play, too?" Ryan asked once, mouth full of cake. Viv smiled as though amused by the idea. "Oh no, darling. Elaina's not dressed for the occasion."

I looked down at myself—my old, patched-up dress, sleeves uneven, hem frayed. Viv had told me to wear it "so you don't ruin anything nice."

The other children laughed at my outfit.

Later, when the house was once again empty, and I was clearing away the trash, I found a small ribbon, a pink and soft one, and my heart immediately lurched. Jezzy had dropped it. I, feeling excited, tied it into my hair to see how it looked, and ran into a window to see my reflection.

Viv found me like that.

"So," she said quietly, making me jump, "you think you're Jezzy now?"

Before I could answer, Viv's hand came down hard, yanking the ribbon free.

"This isn't yours, you hear me?"

She tossed it in the fire. I watched as the ribbon turned from pink to black, the flames eating it up.

***

I loved the garden. It was the only spot in the house that did not appear to belong to Viv. It was the place of all soft dirt and rustling leaves. I would creep out early, now and then, just to feel the cool earth under my feet before anybody woke up.

One morning, Viv caught me kneeling by the roses.

"Playing in the dirt again?"

I looked up in panic and immediately tried to explain.

"I was just—"

But Viv was having none of it.

"Don't lie to me!"

That afternoon, the garden gate was locked. The key hung from Viv's necklace, swinging like a warning.

"Flowers are for people who've earned beauty," she said. "Not for little thieves."

***

Some cruelties didn't need shouting.

One night, Robert arrived home earlier than usual, which was so rare that it seemed like the house was breathing its last. I sat in a corner of the kitchen where he found me, with my knees pulled up to my chest.

"Oh, she hasn't said anything all day," Viv said, her voice oozing fake concern. "Won't even apologize."

"For what?" Robert asked.

"For spilling milk. Half a jug, wasted."

Robert hesitated, eyes on his daughter's small frame. "She's a child, Viv."

Viv's lips curved. "A child who needs to learn the value of what she's given."

Robert looked away. He wanted to speak, but Viv's gaze stopped him. He left the room.

That night, I ate nothing.

***

Once a month, a letter came from Rose. It was always addressed to me, though Viv read it first.

“Your grandmother asks if you’ve been good,” Viv would say, unfolding the paper slowly. “Shall I tell her the truth?”

I would nod, eyes downcast.

Viv smiled and took a tiny bit of the margin of the letter, enough to draw my attention.

“You have the rest,” she said, giving me the half-page. “Be grateful for what you have.”

The same night, I felt the torn edge with my fingertips. Half a letter. Half a love. It was definitely more than I was used to.

***

Sometimes, Robert lingered at the foot of the stairs when the children were asleep. He’d hear Viv’s voice through the thin walls—the way someone might speak to a pet they hate but still feed.

He’d hear my muffled sobs.

He’d stand there, fists tight, jaw locked. Then, slowly, he’d turn away and climb into bed beside the woman who had hollowed his house and called it home.

He told himself he’d fix it tomorrow. But tomorrow always came too late.

***

All of this went through my troubled mind as I stood there, washing dishes. The dirty water of the dishes was cold now and full of soap and crumbs. I washed every dish to a shine, even though nobody would ever see. My wrinkled and red little hands made a cracking sound at the joints.

The noise of dishes breaking the silence was a sound I had known long enough by heart.

Clink, scrub, rinse, repeat.

The sound of my life.

The house felt too quiet, with Ryan and Jezzy at a party, Robert at work, and Viv in her bedroom, resting. And the silence? I hated it with a passion because they forced my mind to think of matters I couldn't bear thinking about.

Mainly, about my mother, Ruth.

The woman Viv despised.

Viv never let me forget it – "You are despicable just like your mother, girl," she'd say, sometimes in a hiss, sometimes in a whisper meant to sound like pity. Robert never spoke of her at all. And so, my memories of Ruth lived only in fragments – a soft laugh, a warm hand, a lullaby half-remembered.

But then came the farm. The hunger. The crying. The day I begged my mother to save me, and no one came.

The memory still fanged so well – the dry air, the pain in my stomach, the way my body trembled with weakness and hunger. I kept wondering why my father did not stand up for me more.

And now, several years after that, standing at the sink, I still wondered.

One tear rolled down my cheek, falling into the dishwasher and disappearing forever.

I did not even wipe the following one.

I took another plate, scrubbed harder this time, as though I could wash myself clean of everything—the hunger, the words, the unhappiness. But no matter how hard I tried, the feeling remained.

***

The next day changed everything.

It started quietly, without warning. No special signs appeared, no music played – just grown-ups talking softly behind closed doors while Viv's shoes clicked against the floor.

I waited in the hallway, holding my hands together over my apron. I caught bits and pieces of the conversation.

"...leaving soon..."

"...England..."

"...arrangements must be made..."

I heard my father speaking quietly through the door crack. "What should we do with Elaina?"

Viv answered coldly. "Whatever you do, she is not coming to my family home. They're still bitter about her."

I froze inside. Was my father leaving?

But things worked out differently this time.

That night, my father visited my room - something he rarely did. Standing by the door smelling like cigarettes, he watched me sitting on my bed fixing my doll.

"Elaina," he said quietly, "come with me downstairs. There's someone you should meet."

Two women waited in the parlor. The tall one had gray hair and friendly eyes with glasses - Ms. Martin, who knew my father. The other woman was shorter and round-faced, with folded hands and the kindest smile I had ever seen - Mrs. Nicholas.

Robert coughed slightly. “Mrs. Nicholas knows Ms. Martin,” he explained. “She... she’s a teacher at a nearby school.”

I nodded silently, shifting my bare feet on the carpet.

Mrs. Nicholas smiled warmly. “I hear you help out lots around here,” she said. “Do you enjoy reading, Elaina?”

I looked confused. “I never learned how, ma’am.”

Mrs. Nicholas seemed sad for a moment, but stayed kind.

“Well,” she said, “we can fix that.”

Viv stood near the fireplace, quiet but tense, wearing a fake smile. She wouldn’t look at me.

Ms. Martin touched my cheek, moving a curl away. “Your father got a job overseas,” she explained softly. “He’ll be gone awhile, so he wants you somewhere safe where you can learn things.”

I thought about these words slowly.

Safe.

Learn.

Grow.

I had only heard these words from others before.

Looking at my father’s tired face, I asked, “Will you come get me later?”

His pause told me everything.

"I'll send letters," he said finally. "Listen to Mrs. Nicholas. She'll take good care of you."

Mrs. Nicholas stood up and fixed her dress. "We'll handle everything," she promised. "She'll have a real home. School. Hot food. A real shot at life."

Viv laughed sharply. "Good riddance," she said. "I'll miss having help around here."

Everyone heard her nastiness but stayed quiet.

Things happened fast after that. They made some agreements, packed bags, and soon a car waited outside. Viv stayed inside pretending to clean instead of saying goodbye. My father squeezed my shoulder.

"Be good," he whispered. "Do what they tell you."

I nodded, wanting to beg him to stay, but couldn't find the strength. Mrs. Nicholas held out her hand. It felt warm and safe.

"Ready to go?"

I looked back once at the gate. The gray house stood silent, windows staring down while Jezzy laughed somewhere inside. For once, I stared right back without fear, burning every detail into my memory. This house that hurt me so much.

Then I climbed into the car beside Mrs. Nicholas and felt it start moving. Watching trees pass by through the window, feeling wind in my hair, I wondered something new:

Maybe the bad luck wasn't mine to carry.

I was still wrong.

Chapter 6: A New Life

It was late afternoon as we rode in a late-model Volvo, and the journey seemed to go on forever. I sat between Mrs. Nicholas and Ms. Martin, holding my suitcase tightly in my arms. The wheels of the car bumped over rocks as I watched the passing trees and people. I was leaving behind everything I knew, yet I felt a sense of excitement.

Sitting there quietly gave me time to think, and I began to understand why all of this was happening. My father had received an opportunity to go to the United Kingdom, but he could only take Viv with him for the time being. None of his children would be going with him at that moment, and he was relieved to have found someone like Mrs. Nicholas to care for me while he was away. He was grateful that Mrs. Martin had recommended such a respectable woman to take me in. Jezzy and Ryan would remain with Viv's family, since Viv would be traveling with him. My father considered himself fortunate to have friends like Mrs. Martin and Mrs. Nicholas, and he felt confident that, as a teacher like Mrs. Martin, Mrs. Nicholas would provide me with proper care and guidance.

Mrs. Nicholas and her husband couldn't have kids and wanted to adopt a girl my age. When she heard about me, she said she was more than ready to take me in. It all worked out for the adults in the end. My father and Viv could leave for the UK without this burden; Mrs. Nicholas got her kid, and Ms. Martin felt great that she had helped someone out.

No one asked what I thought.

The quiet shunning was familiar by then, so it barely bothered me. Ms. Martin kept saying it would be a better life with better chances, while Mrs. Nicholas said nothing. I just sat there, listening to her. I was really hoping that I was heading for a better life, because my life until then had been nothing short of hell itself.

I looked out the window, trying to conjure happy thoughts. Pretty and exciting visions flashed in my mind about the UK. According to a few words from my dad and the news, it was a nice place. There were lovely houses, neat streets, and good schools.

I remembered Jezzy and Ryan. Before long, they would be in that nicer land, dressed in new clothes, having fun, and going to a better school, with Viv looking after them. The idea brought tears to my eyes. They were moving away for a better life, and I was being taken to live with strangers. It was as if I was being passed around, given from one person to the next. And yes, it was clear: I was a burden. Viv had made sure to make me feel that way.

The car continued its trek along the rocky road, the air stinging my nose. My hands stayed around my suitcase as I gripped it for dear life. It was giving me some semblance of control.

"My dear, you haven't spoken a single word since we left," Ms. Martin said not unkindly, "You must be missing your family."

I didn't say anything, just kept my gaze down.

"You must be nervous," she said, smiling now, "It will be all right, dear. Mrs. Nicholas is a good woman. She will take good care of you."

Mrs. Nicholas did not look at me as she replied. "Yes. You'd be a good girl, won't you?"

I nodded this time because I didn't want to come off as impolite to the woman who was adopting me and bringing me to her home.

As the silence returned in the carriage, I sneaked some glances at Mrs. Nicholas. She was going to be the third mother figure in my life. I do not remember the first one, my mother. The second one was Viv, and she hated me so clearly that I expected nothing but harsh words and abuse from her. Now there was Mrs. Nicholas...

I wondered what she would feel about me when she really knew me. Would she regard me as a liability, as Viv did? Or would she treat me like a child to love? The idea was too big to digest. I had not experienced love in a long time.

Mrs. Nicholas seemed like a nice person. Her appearance told me that, and so did her voice, which was warm. Her eyes did not have any begrudging look. I wanted to believe this – that she was as nice as she looked. I tried to figure that out by stealing glances at her.

Viv had never been nice. Her cold heart was just as cold as her round face. Even the way Mrs. Nicholas smiled was different. I was hoping that Mrs. Nicholas would be much kinder to me, although she had a stern look.

I held on to that small hope even more as I looked at her for longer. It's possible that she was as good as she seemed. Things might have been going to be different from now on.

Mrs. Nicholas lived in a very nice community with nicely landscaped yards. As I looked at my new house, the sun hit my face. A big house stood there, painted in colors that reminded me of a sunset. The garden back home wasn't half as nice as this yard—flowers lined up perfectly, like soldiers. Not a weed in sight. My father's place was bigger, but the community was not as nice. My brain felt fuzzy trying to take it all in.

Finally, the car stopped, and Mrs. Nicholas hopped out first, fixing her dress like she always did, a habit I'd noticed during the ride. She looked at her house as if it were her baby. Ms. Martin got out next and reached back to help me. I waited around, hoping Mrs. Nicholas would take my hand like normal mothers did with their kids.

That didn't happen.

My nose caught the mix of roses and wet paint. Some birds were making a racket nearby. It was a very nice place, but I couldn't properly digest it because my stomach was doing backflips.

I watched Mrs. Nicholas walk ahead to the driveway, to the front door. Back straight as a ruler, hat perfectly balanced, like she'd practiced walking that way. I ran to catch up, scared she'd forget about me before I even saw inside.

She kind of twisted around at the door.

"Keep up, dear," she said, all proper but kind of coldly. She disappeared inside, leaving Ms. Martin and me to follow her.

I stumbled in after her, not used to the slippery floors because they weren't there back home. Books and pictures covered almost every wall space I saw. The living room was nicer than anything I had ever seen. A peaceful silence garbed it. I wrinkled my nose at the smell of polish. The curtains were letting the sunlight in, making everything look dreamy.

The living room looked quaint. A peaceful silence garbed it. There was only one person there. An old man is sitting in a large chair near the window. He held a folded newspaper in his hands and looked up when we entered. His hair was thin and gray, and his face was lined and serious.

I knew at once that this was Mr. Nicholas.

He did not greet us. Rather, he stared over the top of his newspaper. His gaze was fixed on me. His eyes were pale and cold. Something in that look felt wrong. It made me shrink where I stood. This was not a curious look. It was not polite. It felt like a harsh judgment. It felt like something much heavier.

I grabbed my sleeve and quickly dropped my head. I hoped he would finally look away. My heart pounded hard in my chest. I desperately wished Ms. Martin would speak. I needed her to fill the empty silence. She said nothing. She only smiled at me instead.

"That's Mr. Nicholas, Elaina," she said kindly. "This is your new home. You will be a good girl and listen to her, won't you?"

I nodded quickly. "Yes, ma'am," I said in a small voice.

Mrs. Nicholas smiled at that, her eyes kind but a little tired.

"That's a good girl," she said. "You must be tired from the journey. We'll get you settled soon."

Mr. Nicholas said nothing. He lowered his eyes to his newspaper again and gave a small shake of his head.

A pregnant pause followed. Ms. Martin looked between them, then back at me.

"You'll be all right here," she said, forcing another smile. "Mrs. Nicholas will take good care of you."

I nodded once more, but my stomach was tight.

Ms. Martin touched me on the shoulder. "Be brave, dear," she muttered, and swiveled about and faced Mrs. Nicholas. "I'll leave now. Good day."

Mrs. Nicholas walked away with her. I stood in the hall, and I looked through the gap as Ms. Martin opened the door, waved one hand, and disappeared down the path.

Mrs. Nicholas brought me into the living room again. The atmosphere was cool, and smelled of the over-finished furniture. She pointed to a cushioned chair in one corner of the room.

"Sit down, Elaina," she said.

I did so, as I was asked, clasping my hands together in my lap. The chair was comfortable, but I sat on the edge of it, too anxious to recline.

"You won't cause any trouble, will you?" Mrs. Nicholas looked at me kindly.

I shook my head quickly. "No, ma'am."

Her smile widened a little. "No more 'ma'am,' dear. You will call me Auntie from now on. And Mr. Nicholas, you may call him Uncle. All right?"

I nodded again, my hands clasping even tighter together. "Yes, Auntie."

She seemed pleased. "Good girl," she said.

For a moment, everything was quiet except for the slow ticking of the clock on the wall. But the longer I sat there, the more uneasy I felt. Something in the air made my skin prickle. It was the feeling of being watched.

I lifted my head slightly and saw why.

Mr. Nicholas, or Uncle, was gazing round at me from his newspaper. The only thing that I could see was his creepy eyes. He did not blink much. He was merely staring at me, as though I were an object which he had not quite made out.

When Auntie sat across from him, he stopped staring.

"You see, dear," she mused, with worry in her voice, "it is such a shame that this child has never been to school. Eight years old, and she can barely read or write. How she has lived so long without being sent to school, I can't even imagine."

Uncle made a sound between a laugh and a grunt.

"She'll have to go to school while she's with us. We can't have a child living here who doesn't even know how to read."

Auntie agreed but said nothing more. She picked up her tea, took a sip, real slow, like she was buying time, and just started talking about something else. Lesson plans. The kids at school. The church. Anything but *me*.

I stayed quiet. Hands in my lap, and my eyes mostly down. But I kept glancing at Uncle. He never looked back, not once. Still, I could feel that cold spot in the room where his attention had been.

He was supposed to be my new dad temporarily.

But he didn't say hi or even my name, and he didn't bother to fake a smile. He just gave me that long, quiet look, like I was something he'd found under the sink. It made me want to vanish right then and there.

My real father? Yeah, he messed up. A lot. Looked away when he should've stepped in. Stayed quiet when he should've roared. But I always knew—*knew*—he loved me.

This man—Uncle—was indifferent toward me. I wasn't sure what to expect from him, but I had a premonition that I was going to have problems with him. I felt it in my bones before he even said a single word.

After dinner—I'd eaten alone at that little kitchen table, pushing food around like it owed me money—Mrs. Nicholas called me. "Come on," she said, not unkindly, but like it was already decided. "Let's get you upstairs."

The hallway was brightly lit, and smelled like soap and something flowery—lilac, maybe? Or just old perfume. She stopped at this door in the corner, turned the knob.

"This is your room," she said, opening it wide. "What do you think?"

I stepped in slowly.

It was small, but clean. A cot against the wall with a white sheet, blanket folded at the foot like in a hospital. A dresser next to it, wood polished till it shone under the lamp. Walls are painted this pale cream color.

I just stood there, with growing excitement. I never dreamed that I would have my own room, especially one like this!

Back home, where I slept, was not a room. Viv turned a storage closet into my space because it was "convenient." Jezzy and Ryan got real bedrooms; beds, curtains, and space to move. Mine? Piled with broken chairs, old boxes, junk nobody wanted. I used to sleep curled up in the gaps, careful not to breathe too hard in case something crashed down.

This place… it wasn't home. But it didn't feel like a punishment either. Just… empty. And for once, that emptiness didn't scare me. It just sat there, waiting.

This room, though simple, felt different. The air was clean. The blanket smelled fresh. There was nothing broken or thrown away. It looked like a real room made for a real person.

Mrs. Nicholas watched me from the doorway. "Do you like it, Elaina?" she asked again.

I nodded. And smiled – the first smile of the day.

"Yes, Auntie," I said. "It is nice."

She smiled back, pleased with my answer. "Good. You can unpack your things and rest. You must be tired from the journey."

I placed my small suitcase on the dresser and touched the blanket with my hand. It was soft and smooth.

This room was not grand, but it was mine. For the first time in a long while, I had a place where I could sleep without the smell of dust and broken wood.

Mrs. Nicholas stood at the door before leaving me for the night.

"Tomorrow," she said, "you will be starting your study."

The words sounded strange to my ears. I repeated them in my mind, not sure what they truly meant. Before, I had not been to school. I was kept at home to clean and do the housework while other kids went to school and had fun. The concept of learning was almost like a new thing to me, as if it were a word from someone else's world.

After putting on my pajamas that evening, I quietly went into the little bed. The cover seemed nice and gentle to my skin. I stared at the ceiling, which was light and strange. The house was silent, and the only thing that could be heard was the ticking of a clock that was somewhere in the corridor.

I thought about what school might be like. I remembered Jezzy and Ryan back home, getting ready each morning. They would dress in clean uniforms and pack their bags with books and pencils. Jezzy would brag about her handwriting or laugh about something her teacher said. Ryan would talk about numbers and the games they played at school. I used to watch them from the corner, pretending not to listen, while Viv brushed their hair and praised them.

I had always wondered what they learned inside those classrooms. I had seen the books my father read sometimes, the ones with words running across the pages like little black rivers. He had said books had stories, and knowledge, and dreams. I would think about how it would be to read one on my own, know all the words, and be aware of things as other people were.

When I lay there in my new room, I wondered about letters and numbers, chalk and slates, and sitting at a desk and writing my name for the first time. My heart ached faster because of the thought.

I was in an unfamiliar house among people whom I barely knew. All the things around me were new and unfamiliar. Yet a feeling was waking somewhere warm in the depths of my soul. At the beginning, it was little, like a spark that had long been waiting to be seen.

I felt something I had almost forgotten for the first time in years.

I felt hopeful.

***

A knock on the door woke me the next morning.

“Elaina,” Mrs. Nicholas’s voice came from the other side. “Time to get up, dear. Breakfast is ready.”

I opened my eyes slowly, blinking against the pale morning light that filled the room. For a moment, I had to remind myself where I was. The bed beneath me was soft. The smell in the air was clean. This was not the small storage room back home. This was my new room in a strange house.

I rolled out of bed, made my blanket flat, and slipped the dress on, which was presented to me by Mrs. Nicholas the previous night. My hands trembled slightly. I was nervous about seeing the adults one more time. I had no idea what they expected from me or what the rules of this house were.

Gingerly, I turned the knob and walked into the corridor. The house radiated serenity. At the far end of the corridor, the sunbeams were lighting through the window, and from somewhere in the corridor, I could hear the sound of dishes being moved. As I was climbing down the stairs, a warm smell reminiscent of butter caught my attention. My stomach echoed a quiet protest.

I went to the doorway of the kitchen, and I paused. The room was sunny and full of delicious smells. Mrs. Nicholas was at the stove, heating a pot and humming to herself. The table was already laid with plates and glasses. For the first time, no one told me to watch the stove or fetch a broom as soon as I entered. Mrs. Nicholas turned when she saw me and smiled kindly.

"Good morning, Elaina," she said. "Come, take a seat. Breakfast is almost ready."

I nodded, still unsure, and moved carefully toward the table. Mr. Nicholas was already sitting there with his newspaper. He did not greet me. He only glanced at me before looking back down at the page.

I got a weird sensation. His presence made the air colder.

I sat in a chair opposite him, so that I did not have to sit too close. The food on my plate looked delicious just by its appearance. Steam was coming out of the eggs, and there was bread, with butter melting on it. The orange juice beside it was glowing like gold in the morning sunlight.

My fork and I got hold of a small bite. The food was rich and soft, which was not common for me. It tasted good in my mouth, yet on the other hand, it was also weird, nearly excessive. My stomach was not sure what to do with such food. I slowed down my chewing, tasting both comfort and wood at the same time. Mrs. Nicholas was seated opposite me with a plate of her own. She smiled frequently when she was eating and addressed me in a light voice.

"You must eat well, Elaina," she said. "A growing girl needs her strength."

This was the usual routine for breakfast, except on weekends, when Mrs. Nicholas would prepare a more lavish meal. Mrs. Nicholas often told me, "You are welcome here, dear," she would say warmly. "We have wanted a daughter for so long. It felt like a blessing when Ms. Martin told us about you." She turned slightly toward her husband. "Don't you agree, dear?"

Mr. Nicholas nodded without speaking; he never made comments when she tried to reassure me that they were happy to have me.

That first week, Mrs. Nicholas sat me down and explained what was expected of me. I listened carefully because I wanted her to be pleased with me.

"First," she said, "you need to be respectful to your uncle and me. We do not expect you to talk back when given instructions. Secondly, you must keep your room and the rest of the house in order. Your main chores will be washing the dishes and keeping your room tidy. You must also do your homework without being told."

She smiled again. "And last, you must always be polite. Speak kindly, listen to the adults, and everything will go well."

I nodded, folding my hands in my lap. "Yes, Auntie," I said softly.

"The rules are simple, aren't they?" she asked.

"Yes, Auntie."

The rules did not seem that hard. After all, I had lived with far worse.

From the first week, Mrs. Nicholas began tutoring me in a room that resembled an office, with books neatly stacked on the shelves. The air carried a faint scent of paper and tea.

I was nervous about my first session, since I had never been to school before. I didn't know what to expect, but she began by saying, "I will assist you at home with reading so that you will be at a certain level when you start school. You'll be attending the school where I teach, so proper conduct and academic achievements are required. You cannot be an embarrassment to me, since I teach there."

My first tutoring session with Mrs. Nicholas went very well. She explained that the first thing I needed to learn was the vowels. She started by asking me to make the vowel sounds A, E, I, O, and U. After that, she taught me words, their definitions, and how to use them in sentences. She was amazed at how quickly I grasped the concepts, and within two months, I was reading very well.

"You are a fast learner," she said after a while. "You have never been to school, but you have a smart head on you."

I was surprised at the words. I stared at her for a moment. I never had anyone talk to me in that way. Viv had only called me names. My father had hardly said anything. Being told I was smart felt strange but good. Something warm spread inside me, and a smile grew on my face before I realized it.

Mrs. Nicholas noticed. "That's better," she said. "A child who enjoys learning should smile. It means she is ready to grow."

I nodded. "Yes, Auntie."

Amazingly, within six months, I had become an avid reader. I developed a fondness for *Mills and Boon* novels, and instead of doing my chores, I would hide away and read. Reading quickly became my favorite hobby—it was my solace.

Chapter 7: My First School Escapades

After some time, Mrs. Nicholas told me it was okay to start school. Things got harder for me after two years at St. Albans, the school where Mrs. Nicholas taught. Time went by quickly. In addition to Mrs. Nicholas's class, I had classes with other teachers for different subjects.

My issues started with my peers. Two years later, I was very different from before. I had turned into a neat, sure of herself, young lady who started to look pretty good. My skin care and hairstyle skills improved. I started to speak English correctly and cared more about how I dressed. After learning more about fashion, I wanted to look my best.

Some of the girls in my class did not like how I had changed, which was sad. They became mean to me and made fun of me. I was bullied because they thought I *acted* as if I was better than them. Sadly, they held on to this belief during my entire time at the school.

Everything finally got out of hand one afternoon when a group of girls surrounded me in the girls' bathroom. They stood around me, laughing and talking, with angry faces. They looked like they were ready to fight, and I knew I had to decide quickly. I took a deep breath and looked at them very carefully. That's when I knew I had to do something to stop what was happening, and that something was to deal with the leader of the group.

After that thought, I stood my ground and realized that the only way to end the bullying was to make an example of Tami, the group leader.

While I was thinking that, she made it easy for me by sticking her finger in my face. At that point, I taught her that she should not judge a book by its cover because I was not the wimp she thought I was. The other students were shocked and quickly moved away. They found out that day that I wasn't someone to be pushed around, even though they thought I was too "uppity."

Following that episode, there was no more bullying. The girls who used to make fun of me started to be cautious around me, and some even made an effort to be kind. I eventually gained a few close friends who appreciated my ability to advocate for myself. Knowing that I could defend myself when necessary made me feel stronger and more self-assured after that day.

I started purchasing lunch and ice cream for these new acquaintances at school because I wanted to keep them. I didn't want to lose the positive feeling that came with being accepted. I initially thought it would be okay to utilize my own lunch money. However, when my funds eventually ran out, I started utilizing Mrs. Nicholas's funds instead.

This went on for a while, and to be honest, I didn't think anyone would ever notice. I continued doing it because my pals were content and I liked spending time with them. But one day, when one of my instructors told Mrs. Nicholas how giving I had been at school, always purchasing snacks and treats for my peers, everything changed. Mrs. Nicholas became suspicious after that innocuous remark and quickly started questioning how I could buy all those items.

The result was anything but nice. Mrs. Nicholas became enraged upon learning about it, and the issue swiftly spread across the school. Consequently, several of us were chosen to receive punishment. We were lined up and given four strokes on the palms of our hands with the cane used for discipline, though it's still unclear why the other pupils were also disciplined. Each strike caused a searing pain, and I recall fighting back tears as my hands ached. I learnt a difficult lesson that day, and my generosity was undoubtedly over.

I did everything I could to avoid trouble after that episode. When I attended Mrs. Nicholas's Junior Secondary school, there weren't many more significant problems. Life became more routine as things calmed down. The true drama started when I transferred to the senior school two years later. There, I faced an entirely new set of difficulties.

Senior school life was different from junior secondary school. The pupils were older, more self-assured, and had a wider range of interests. At that point, I began to attract the attention of boys. They would grin at me in the corridor, try to converse, and occasionally give me small notes via my pals.

Mrs. Nicholas soon noticed that I was growing up and had become a young lady. She sat me down one day and had a very serious discussion with me about my becoming a teenager. It was very important for her to tell me to be careful about boys and men. No matter what they said or promised, she told me not to let boys or men touch me. I knew she meant every word.

I thought about what she said after we spoke. I tried not to notice the boys at school and kept my attention on my work. Some girls laughed and talked about their boyfriends, but I remembered the discussion with Mrs. Nicholas about what I should not do to stay out of trouble.

The girls in my classes started to be jealous, like they had been in middle school. The only change was that I was a teenager now and looked better. Some of the girls called me "Miss World" because they thought I was acting "uppity." Soon, people began to gossip about me as they did at my previous school.

The scenario was the same, with a group leader who instigated fights. I was always challenged to get physical, but I was careful not to get caught up, because if we were caught fighting, especially more than once, we would be suspended from school.

As the school years went on, two memorable things happened that I will never forget. The first one was pretty serious, but now that I think about it, it's kind of funny. Our male teacher chose to take our class to a place called Mineral Bath for a field trip. Everyone was excited to swim and have fun at this spot with a big pool.

When I saw the pool, I became excited and decided to enter. While entering, I stepped on the next-to-last step instead of the last one, which caused me to fall. I fell over into the water and couldn't get back on my feet. As I struggled to stay above the water, I began to drown. The thing that shocked me the most was that a girl from my class did nothing but watch me, smiled, and said, "Patricia, why don't you get out of the pool? Don't you see that you're drowning?"

At that time, a male student brushed against me just as I was going under for the third time. I shot straight up in the water. He was shocked. "What are you doing?" he asked me. "Are you not aware that you were drowning?"

My teacher was a man, and more boys than girls were in the class. It was strange and depressing that none of the girls who were standing by thought to call the teacher or ask for help. The names of those two kids still stick out in my mind.

The second event was more traumatic for me, even more so than my near-drowning. There was a fair at the Senior school, and Mrs. Nicholas was asked to help even though she didn't work there. Every once in a while, I had to ask her when she was ready to leave. She told me she wasn't ready yet, the last time I checked with her.

A cute kid I liked asked me to dance while I was waiting. I agreed because I was glad and excited. We had only been dancing for a short time when Mrs. Nicholas walked up to me out of the blue, in front of everyone, snuck up behind me, and gave me two loud slaps on my back.

I've never felt so embarrassed in my whole life as at that moment. I was so ashamed that my face hurt, and I wished the ground would open up and swallow me up. The shame stuck with me for a long time. I can still feel how bad that day was when I think about it now. Everything about my relationship with Mrs. Nicholas changed after that. In fact, it took a terrible turn.

Chapter 8: Events Before My Father's Return

Things continued as usual at school. I called myself dating one of the popular boys, although it wasn't really dating because he couldn't come to my home, nor could I go anywhere with him. We just exchanged notes in class, telling each other how much we liked each other, while the other boys and girls acted as if we were off limits.

I eventually got three girlfriends at school. One of them was on the wilder side, with a boyfriend who was much older than her. Then, to make things interesting, I would accompany her after school in the evenings to visit this man. During one of these visits, her boyfriend introduced me to one of his friends, who took a liking to me.

Now, this was very interesting because I recalled the warnings from Auntie, telling me to stay away from boys and grown men. Fortunately, the young man, Bobby, was ethical and did not try to get involved with me because I was a young teenager. Over the years, I reflected on that period and thought about how wrong my life could have turned out if I had been in that unhealthy situation.

My friend got pregnant, and I really can't remember what the outcome was, but I do recall that she had many issues with this young man. Although I did not dare to tell her, I thought she was doing too much at her age, and I often wondered why her mother allowed this.

So while I was developing real friendships at school, my home life took a turn for the worse.

My behavior became rebellious after the incident with Mrs. Nicholas at the fair. I started to despise Mrs. Nicholas. I would take a long time to do my chores by locking myself in the bathroom and reading for hours. Mrs. Nicholas would bang on the door, but I would not answer. When I finally emerged, she asked, "What have you been doing in the bathroom for so long? And why have you not finished cleaning the house?"

My response was usually hostile: "I am going as fast as I can. I am not a machine."

Her usual response was always, "How dare you speak to me like that?"

She would then begin to slap me around, but that did not make any difference because I would do it again.

She acted as if she did not know the reason for the change in my behavior, or if she did, I guess she did not care. But I know that it was because of what she did to me at the fair.

Things escalated beyond the incident at the fair one Saturday morning. I was washing dishes when Mrs. Nicholas appeared, took a plate, and examined it.

Suddenly, she gave me a huge slap. "Do you call this plate clean?"

Up until this day, I am still surprised at my action because I slapped her in her face.

Oh, my goodness, she was in a state of shock just as I was. She yelled, "You little wretch, you slapped me?"

She immediately pushed me outside and told me, "You will never put your foot back in my house!"

I stayed outside the rest of the day without food, but fortunately, she allowed me back in the house when it became dark. I was not proud of what I did, but later in life, I realized that I inherited that from my father, who was a no-nonsense type of person. This is the reason why I am so confused about the way he allowed Viv to control him during the early years of my life.

Along with my growing dislike for Mrs. Nicholas, I had a nagging displeasure with the fact that she had me traveling on the bus with a basket on Fridays. I was so outraged that I was wearing my school uniform, and some of my peers rode the same bus.

Once, a girl my age asked me, "Why is she allowing you to take this basket? Couldn't she use a regular shopping bag?"

"I know," I responded. "She thinks she is too good to carry the basket, but it's okay for me to take it on my way to school. Girl, I am beginning to really dislike her."

My taking the basket on Friday mornings affected my pride, but taking it home affected me physically. Mrs. Nicholas was so selfish and mean that she would fill the basket at the market and give it to me to carry. The wicked woman would carry the smallest number of packages and give me the heaviest to carry. The basket was so heavy that I often had to carry it on my head.

The neighborhood had a group of boys who were always admiring me. When we got off the bus on those Friday nights, they would assist me with the basket if they were hanging out. I was even more embarrassed because I had a crush on one of these boys.

Unknown to me, during my growing unhappiness with Mrs. Nicholas, there would soon be another change in my life.

Mrs. Nicholas had a beautiful niece named Ditty, who, for some unknown reason, had to stay with her while she finished her last year of high school. After dinner one evening, Mrs. Nicholas told me that Ditty would be sharing my room.

"Wow, this is exciting!" I told her. I was happy because I thought it would be nice to have someone close to my age living with us.

Just as I thought, living with Ditty was fun. I was able to tell her about many things that bothered me about living with her aunt. In turn, Ditty told me what was bothering her while she was there. Uncle—he was her problem. It seemed that Uncle had been making passes at her. She didn't tell me the full details, but her stay was short-lived. I was devastated when she told me she was leaving immediately after her graduation.

I became very sad and asked her why she was leaving.

"I cannot afford to be pregnant by an old man," she said.

I was confused, but she didn't explain further. However, I realized it was because of Uncle. I then started to recall the times I had caught him near her with that sneaky look on his face. Ditty left a week after her graduation.

To this day, I still think about her sometimes. Many years later, I learned that she migrated to Canada, got married, and had children.

Apart from getting an education and developing into a charming, attractive young lady, my life with Mrs. Nicholas was very boring. The highlight of my life was reading Mills and Boon novels, going on the occasional school field trips, and attending fairs and street dances in the neighborhood. The street dances were really nice, and I was fortunate to be allowed to go. But being able to attend these events came with a price—I had to complete all my chores properly and on time.

Well… this mundane life would have continued, but the next events of my life were about to unfold.

After Ditty's departure, Uncle started to have his eye on me. He would present himself in the rooms while I was cleaning. He would suddenly start to get close to me, trying to hold my hands, and exhibit other creepy behavior. It was an unstated message that whatever he was trying to do should not be reported to Auntie. He would say disturbing things like "You don't have to be afraid, just sit on my lap."

Of course, I would put up a fight and tell him I am doing nothing of the sort. However, his persistence in trying to molest me got on my nerves, and just as I was about to tell Auntie, there was a divine intervention, or so I thought at that time.

I will never forget the day Mrs. Nicholas told me that my father was back from the UK and wanted to see me. Wow, I was so excited. The plan was for me to visit on Saturday afternoon and return on Sunday, so I could go to school on Monday. When I got to the house, my father was impressed with the young lady I had become. I was well spoken, literate, and very attractive.

"Elaina, is that you? You have grown so much and are now so intelligent," he said.

Viv did not hide her surprise and jealousy very well. Her only comment was, "Well, I guess Mrs. Nicholas did take care of you."

My father, still basking in pleasure, replied, "She certainly did."

All the excitement and my ego being stroked led me to make a very foolish decision. That decision was not to return to Mrs. Nicholas but to stay with my father. Viv was happy about that because, upon seeing me, she immediately began to think about having me as her maid to help with the two children she had while in the UK. So, of course, she agreed that I should not return to Mrs. Nicholas.

However, Mrs. Nicholas and her husband were very angry about my father taking me back because the agreement was for them to have me permanently. Looking back on the decision I made, I know that if Mrs. Nicholas had not been as mean as she was and her husband had not shown the tendencies of a child molester, I would have stayed. Yes, I was fed and sent to school, but my emotional health was never addressed.

Chapter 9: The Last Years with Viv and My Father

Well… the glorious times I envisioned after my father's return were just a delusion. Viv wasted no time reverting to her old vicious ways, but this time it was a different ball game entirely. She was now dealing with a new Elaina, a fact she realized very early.

It was now evident to Viv that stopping me from going to school would never be a possibility. I attended school as usual, continued to take care of my appearance, and kept up with my studies. Focusing on school at that point was crucial because I was preparing to graduate, with the goal of entering a Technical High School. I already had in mind which Technical School I would attend.

Things progressed, with me earning good grades, making new friends in the neighborhood, and planning for my graduation. Viv had me doing a lot of chores, but at that point, the real viciousness had not yet kicked in. My father was a very stingy man. As the saying goes, "He does not give away prayers." Because of his stinginess, it was very hard to get the perfect dress for my graduation. However, I managed to find a very nice, simple dress. Needless to say, it was simple, but I looked good in it. A graduation should be a child's greatest memory, but to this day, I cannot recall if my father attended. Of course, Viv did not attend, but I am not sure if my father did. If he had, that memory would be etched in my mind. But I do remember that I looked nice and had a very good time.

Unfortunately, that evening was the last time I saw any of my peers from that school. I did see a girl who had been a close friend, her name was Lorna, but after a few years, we completely lost contact.

Was my life "rosy" after graduation? Heck no! This was the moment I truly saw who Viv really was. After graduation, I handed my father the paperwork about the school I planned to attend, since I had also passed the entrance exam. He took this information to Viv, and her outraged response was, "Why would you want to send her back to school? I need her to help me with the children." The children she mentioned were the two girls she had in the UK.

So what did my weak, manipulated father do? He came back to me with this statement: "Elaina, Viv thinks it's best if you do not go back to school because she needs you to help with Del and Delilah." I was now in the second and final stage of abuse from Viv and my enabling father. Viv instantly laid out all the chores I would be responsible for, and they were basically everything needed to keep the home running. At this point, all the children she had were back and living with them. The two youngest girls, the ones she had in the UK, returned wearing diapers the size of towels, and washing them was also my responsibility.

But that was only one of the hideous tasks that were thrust upon me. I was responsible for cleaning the entire house, which was quite large; washing and ironing my father's uniforms; washing sheets and all the household chores; and cooking.

And what did the evil stepmother do? There was a couple across the street from our house, and Viv was very close with them. Apparently, she was closer to the husband, because every day, as soon as my father and the neighbor's wife left for work, Viv would position herself at the window facing our house. She would disappear for a while, but then return and sit there until it was time for my father to come home. This continued for a very long time.

During all this misery, however, something wonderful happened. My father connected with my sister, who was born the month after I was. She was excited to connect with her father, but she soon realized how blessed she was to have been living with her grandmother, since her mother was deceased. She was very smart and was doing very well in high school.

My father convinced her to spend the summer with us. I enjoyed her visit, but she decided that one visit was enough. She did not like what she observed during her stay, and Viv was certainly not her favorite person.

Well, I continued to be the maid for quite some time until the good Lord intervened. This intervention came about when a cousin of mine came to visit. He was appalled at what he saw. I had the opportunity to tell him about my desire to go back to school, but I was unable to do so because of the lack of funds and my father's reluctance to help me.

He told me he thought I had potential and that he would assist me. Wow, I was flabbergasted! However, the greatest hurdle was getting my father to agree, yet God was in charge. I conducted my research and selected a school, as well as the courses I would be taking, before consulting with my father.

When I told him that I was going back to school and explained how it would be paid for, he agreed. But Madam Viv was outraged. Her response was, "I could not have a child going to school and have a man paying for it." I will remember my father's response for the rest of my life: "She will go to school and do the courses she wants to do." That was it. I was only dependent on him for my bus fare. In retrospect, I also think he knew that I would be going to the school whether he agreed or not.

Shortly after I started attending this business school, things began to get very interesting. I chose English, Shorthand, Typewriting, and Switchboard Operating. I performed so well that the school's owner asked me to teach the Switchboard Operating class. Major companies would contact the school to hire their brightest and most promising students.

Because I was doing so well, I was selected to work for a popular company as their Telephone Operator. I was only seventeen years old. The envy and jealousy from Viv were at the boiling point. Of course, she did not expect all this sudden success from a child she had done everything to suppress from an early age.

I had now become a truly refined young lady, wearing very nice clothes and starting to date.

Everything was building toward the final chapter of that turbulent life. Jezzy was also back, but to this day, I don't know whether it was because of her conduct that she returned, since she was supposed to be living with one of Viv's relatives as an adoptive child. Based on the kind of person she turned out to be, I believe it was because of her conduct. Of all the siblings, she created the most mischief by lying and acting as if she were better than everyone else. Ryan was different and did not create conflicts. But Deliah, one of the two born in the UK, later became a monster just as Jezzy.

The catastrophe that led to my leaving the bondage of living with Viv was partly Jezzy's doing. The confrontation stemmed from a lie she told

Viv, and it escalated. I do not recall exactly what caused the argument, but Viv flew into a rage, cursed me, and finally threw a huge vase at me. I must have said something she didn't like, because by then, I was no longer allowing her to degrade me verbally.

The vase did not hit me, but it shattered, and somehow, I got a horrible cut on the bottom of my right foot from the broken glass. The cut was so severe that I could not walk without limping. I might have lost my foot had it not been for the Plant Manager at my job, who had obviously taken a liking to me. He surprised me by asking, "What happened to your foot?" I told him about the incident with Viv and showed him the cut. He was appalled. "You'll have to go to the doctor because that's a very bad cut," I told him. I knew, but I didn't have the money to go to the doctor. "I'll give you the money to go," he said, "because the cut is really bad."

The doctor confirmed what he said. "Young lady, if you hadn't come to see me, you would have certainly lost your foot. It's badly infected, and the infection was spreading." I don't recall my father's reaction to the injury, but I do remember that he was displeased when Viv threw the vase, since he was present during the altercation.

This incident reminded me of another violent attack from Viv when I was very young. It was a Sunday, and my father was visiting a neighbor close by. Viv began to berate me about something I no longer remember. What I do remember vividly is that she called me a "little bitch" and threw a knife at me. The knife was aimed at my face, but my guardian angel was with me. It zigzagged and hit me on the left thigh instead. That scar is still visible.

I told my father I would be leaving their home and began apartment hunting. I explained that his wife had a strong hatred for me and that I was no longer willing to endure her abuse.

Thus began the next major chapter of my life.

Chapter 10: My Emergence into Adulthood

Soon, I was able to find a nice home to share, and I purchased a comfortable bedroom set and other essentials that I needed to accommodate my new living arrangement. Also, the rent was reasonable, and the people in the home were a support group.

My belief that the Plant Manager, Lloyd, really liked me was correct. After the healing of my foot, he continued to assist me. A few months after my injury, I celebrated my 18th birthday. Lloyd gave me a very nice birthday party, and this signaled our official dating.

Lloyd was very kind and caring, but the negative part about his character was the fact that he was a womanizer, just like my own father. The big difference was that Lloyd took care of his responsibilities. However, his escapades were more sophisticated and daring than my dad's.

I would frequently go down to the plant where he managed, and I would look up and see a young lady looking at me with meanness. When it got to be bad, I asked him about the situation; I even got the girl's name.

"Lloyd, why is Blossom looking at me in such a hostile way when I come into the plant?"

His responses were usually dismissive, until one day she called me, telling me, "Dutty gal, leave my man."

Unbeknownst to her, I connected the call to his extension, and he heard her. The gravity of the situation became clear to me when I discovered that she was living with him. I later learned from one of his relatives that she received a very unpleasant backlash from him because of that action.

Now, here is where things began to get complicated.

I got pregnant!

He was excited. But the strangest thing was that I had a passion for babies; I would admire them on the buses or anywhere I saw them.

Sadly, I could not see the full ramifications of having a child out of wedlock and how it would affect my life. This became evident after I started working in places like banks and other large institutions. Having a child out of wedlock did not affect my ability to get jobs, as I was very attractive and consistently performed well in interviews, which ultimately led to me securing the positions.

The problem was the culture I was born into—a culture that judged people by their neighborhoods, their families, appearance, and occupations.

So, I had my beautiful daughter, Natalia. She was a pretty baby and is now a beautiful woman. Unfortunately, from the age of two onward, she was subjected to very rigid parenting. Although I did love her, I was unable to openly demonstrate that love because I was deprived of affection as a young child.

Nonetheless, she was given everything that I was not given. Her father also took very good care of her. In fact, he "stepped up" when I was three months pregnant because I was fired from the company that he also worked for. This termination came about because my hormones were out of whack, and I would be very rude to the callers.

After my termination, Lloyd would bring me an allowance every Friday; he also took care of my rent and doctor visits. The icing on the cake was that he even paid for me to have Natalia at a private hospital. Did his womanizing stop? Of course not! Ha-ha, he even got another woman in the plant pregnant while Blossom was still working there.

Blossom had very low self-esteem; she tried to fight and harass me. I learned that she was unable to read, so she had her demons and insecurities.

I moved on with my life and decided to travel to the Bahamas because a visa was not required. At that age, I did not have enough stability to obtain a visa for the USA. A memory that will remain with me was when I told Lloyd that I intended to go to the Bahamas.

"Why would you want to go to the Bahamas when the baby is so young?" he had asked.

"I am bored and depressed because I was at home so long without working," I simply replied.

He gave in, but when it got closer to my departure, he came to me with tears in his eyes.

"You mean you cannot wait until Natalia gets older? Please, I am begging you."

I was sad to see this coming from him, but it was too late; everything was already in motion for my departure.

So, I went to the Bahamas, but I stayed for only three months because I became concerned about my daughter, who was left with my grandmother, Rose. Lloyd and I remained very good friends, and he continued to take care of Natalia financially even in my absence. Unfortunately, I became obsessed with traveling and continued to visit the Bahamas.

One interesting aspect of my trips to the Bahamas is that I would pack my furniture and leave it at my father's house, since he had the space. When I returned to the island, I would have to stay at his house until I got another job. This practice, and the first tragedy in my life, put a halt to my traveling to the Bahamas.

After my return from my longest stay in the Bahamas, I went back to my father's house to find my lovely furniture partially destroyed. At this point, all of Viv's children were living at the home except for a daughter who was adopted by a schoolteacher. Unfortunately, Jezzy was also at the house, and she now had a son. He was just a baby when I returned. Living with her was like living in a cage with various species of deadly snakes.

The dramatic incident occurred one morning when I decided to act on a humane impulse. Her baby, a son, was crying a lot. When I looked at him, he was wet and in need of a bath. I said, "Jezzy, the baby needs a bath or at least to be changed."

Her response to me was hostile, although I cannot recall it verbatim.

So, I decided to bathe the baby myself. After the baby's bath, I asked, "Can you take the baby's clothes, the ones I just took off, and the ones lying around, and wash them? They are causing these little flies."

She went into a rage.

After cursing me, she raced out of the yard and located her mother, Viv, who was visiting a neighbor. Her story to her was that I slapped her. That was a blatant lie, and to this day, I remember it vividly.

The outcome of her falsehood came swiftly. After being verbally abused by Viv, the verbal abuse turned into assault. She delivered her story to my father with great confidence, and I challenged each part that twisted the truth. My contradiction enraged her.

She sprang forward with a violence that seemed to come from nowhere and tore a thick lock of my hair.

Luckily, my father was there to intercede. I made it clear to her afterward that any repeat of that attack would be met with a response strong enough to stop her.

I said, "If you try that again, you will regret it, because you will not bite my finger off as you did my mother's."

She screamed, "You bitch, you better get your ass out of this house!" Her voice filled the room with a sharp, bitter anger that came from someplace deeper than the moment itself.

I replied, "I will not be going anywhere until I get a job, then I will gladly leave." My heart was pounding at this point.

My father was supportive then and told her that I could not leave. His tone carried a firmness that settled the room for a brief moment.

Being the blessed person that I was, I found a wonderful job that I remained in until my departure to the USA. I also found a very nice apartment, so my life was back to normal until tragedy struck.

Lloyd and I resumed what might have been dating or just being good friends. However, his life became tragic. The first tragic occurrence was when he was held up and shot.

Thank the Lord he did not die, but he was shot in his right arm and was unable to work. His respect for me was huge because I was so understanding and supportive, while Blossom, with whom he was living, would curse him daily about his inability to work so that she could have money. He continued to be an excellent father to my daughter and even paid for her to attend a private school.

Life went on. He regained his health, married Evil Blossom, had another child with another woman, and continued to be Lloyd. I continued my life, dating, working, and just trying to be happy, and learning how to carry the past without letting it shape every part of my future.

Then came the most horrible day of my life.

It was a Monday morning at work, and although I cannot recall all the details, I received a call that led to the discovery that Lloyd had been killed in a car crash over the weekend.

I was devastated. Yes, we were not together romantically, but he was my daughter's father, and he was a jovial, kind, and helpful person. This was the turning point in my life. I felt that I needed to get away from the country and start a new life. My perspectives were completely changed after Lloyd's death.

Chapter 11:
My Work Life Before USA

As I stated earlier, I was very lucky in getting hired. I had a nice personality and looked attractive. However, I was like a "diamond in the rough."

Although I was good at what I did, there were many areas in my personality that needed development and improvement. I was very sensitive and had a bad temper. I did not fully grasp the concept of diplomacy or how to respond to negative comments without coming across as rude. Of course, being a receptionist and telephone operator, courtesy was a necessity; it was imperative to have those traits.

Over the years, I realized that I have a "no nonsense personality" that usually lets people know how I feel, and that I do not do well with disrespect or being made a fool of. I realized that these traits were inherited from my father. However, at this stage of my life, I can convey my point without being offensive, unless necessary.

I was working with a large bank before I got my dream job with a manufacturing company. The employees at that bank were very snobbish and made me feel "less than." The main reason was the fact that I was an unwed mother.

Being married was the biggest accomplishment for the ladies my age at the bank; they glorified the title "Mrs." Another significant aspect was the neighborhood you lived in, although I lived in a nice one. The prejudice against me was that I was an unwed mother. Did this bother me? Yes, it did. In retrospect, I think that experience fueled my desire to "be all I can be."

In addition to this type of discrimination, there were men in leadership positions who were sexual molesters. I was targeted by two of them. One was the big boss, and the other was in a leadership role. The one in the leadership role had a wife who also worked at the bank. Undoubtedly, I had nothing to do with him, plus his wife was not a very nice person, nor was he.

I normally walked a specific route to get to my father's home, which required walking across a bridge. The surrounding area was not nice, but it got me to my father's house quickly.

On one of those trips, I saw the individual whose wife worked at the bank. I wondered what he was doing in that neighborhood, but I dismissed the thought, as it wasn't my business. Well… what did he do? I guess he must have told his wife, because the rumor circulated in the bank that I was living in this ghetto neighborhood. I noticed that the snobbishness became worse, and I began to feel like an outcast.

I adjusted to this atmosphere since I needed my job.

Then came the final blow.

The boss called me to his office one afternoon. I was worried, wondering if I was going to be fired. To my surprise, when I got upstairs to his office, what occurred remains with me to this day.

"How are you doing?" he asked.

"I am doing okay," I just said.

Small talk continued until he finally gave me an address where I should meet him after work. I was shocked, but I regained my composure and pleasantly left his office.

I did not go to the address to meet him.

Two or three weeks passed, and then a complaint arose that I had been disrespectful to a caller. Termination was brought up, but the final decision was left up to the big boss.

When I went to his office, and before the allegations were laid out, he asked, “Why did you not turn up?”

I don’t recall what my excuse was, but he told me, “You did not show up as I told you to, so there is nothing I can do for you; you are terminated.”

Looking back on that incident, I realize that I reacted differently when I was younger compared to how I would have handled it later in life. I did not cry or become upset; I left his office calmly.

Shortly after, I ended up with my dream job, where I remained until I left for the USA. Were there obstacles at this job? Of course! As usual, I received criticism from the female employees, although I did have a couple of them as friends. I was very close to one, Faye. We would ride to work together in the mornings and evenings.

The place had many male workers; unfortunately, I got into what might be perceived as a “love triangle.” Regardless, I corrected my mistakes and left the company with my dignity intact. I got promoted on the job, and the vicious females insinuated that I did not achieve it based on performance, but on relationships. To this day, I remember the face of that demonic female who made that allegation, although I will not mention her name.

I recall all the viciousness I endured from the jealous females, and, sadly, from some of the males whose enjoyment was gossiping and tearing other people down. Regardless of the negativity, I enjoyed working for the company. The management was great; they treated all employees with respect and kindness.

I am fortunate enough to still have my last boss as a friend. He is an outstanding man, whom we referred to as Smithy.

Regardless of the occasional friction we sometimes experienced as coworkers, we also had a lot of fun. We would hang out on Fridays when we got paid and party. Another thing that added to the fun was to go out for lunch in groups of three or four and extend our one-hour lunch break. Our bosses were understanding, so we didn't get in trouble or have to make up the time. Now, isn't that something to reminisce about? Where else could we get away with coming back from lunch an hour late, and quite frequently at that? Aww, those good old days!

Well…getting away with coming back late from lunch was not my sole reason for being so fond of the company. Haha…we got paid monthly, and by the middle of the month, we would be asking for a salary advance.

Did we get it? Of course we did!

But my personal appreciation for the management is the fact that they were instrumental in my receipt of my first "Visitor Visa" to the United States. They provided me with an employment letter, as that was a major requirement for the application. They provided me with other pivotal aid, as it was very hard to obtain a visa as a young single female without sufficient ties to demonstrate a reason to return after the visit.

However, I was thrilled to have received the visa and had no intention of abusing it. Hence, my first visit to the great New York City.

Visiting the United States became my vacation destination. I made several trips before deciding that attending college in the United States would be ideal. Lloyd's death also led me to that decision, because strangely, I felt that I had lost a very good friend, and I just got the urge to have a new start. However, the final decision was made after a great deal of prayer and careful consideration of the perfect college in Chicago, Illinois. My daughter joined me at a later date.

Chapter 12: My First Two Years in the USA – Chicago, Illinois

I began my college journey in Chicago, at a college then known as Loop City College, located in the heart of downtown Chicago. Wow, I was very excited and nervous! Here was a challenge to see if I could achieve a college degree. However, I had completed a course in Word Processing before starting my college classes, so I should not have been as nervous.

Worrying was needless. I started with Business Law, and although I changed my major, I learned concepts that have guided me throughout life up to the present day. Most importantly, I became an A student in all my classes, which alleviated any doubts I had about my capabilities.

College was not the only exciting thing that happened to me during those two years in Chicago. I met a young man, whom I shall refer to as Rich. We started dating, but I informed him that after I graduated from college, I would have to return to my country. He asked me to marry him, and I assumed that he cared enough about me to want me to stay in the country.

We had a private wedding, with plans to have a bigger celebration. Unfortunately, this did not materialize. The marriage did not last long due to several factors. We lived in a family home, and his family was not very receptive to me because I was from another country (that was my opinion), especially since they loved a sister-in-law who was American. Secondly, he tried to change careers, and he was very engrossed in that because the process was very difficult for him, with studying and test-taking. Unfortunately, he was unable to spend much time with me, and I was young, left on my own to cope with a new city and a new environment.

A situation that was very disturbing to me was that his mother, stepdad, and sisters lived on the first floor, and they were privy to every argument we had.

An incident occurred one afternoon that confirmed my feelings that they did not like me. Chicago, like New York, has parking on the streets. That evening in question, I had a traffic incident with an African American lady on the street in front of our house. I don't recall all the details, but the lady hit the back of my car. I got out of my car and approached the lady, and asked, "Did you not see me parking right here?" She responded, "You are the dumb bitch that caused the accident."

All I recall is that it was a pretty ugly scene, with the lady almost attacking me. What did Rich's stepdad do? He, his wife, and one of the daughters came to the window and watched everything that was taking place outside on the street. Not one of them came out to see if I was okay or tried to support me. I later found out that they blamed me for the accident. That registered in my mind.

Well, a few months after that incident, the other daughter-in-law, whom they all loved, had a similar incident—only hers escalated more than mine. And what do you think happened? The stepdad and sisters went downstairs to the street, rendered support, and almost attacked the other driver.

My assessment of all the above led me to the decision that I did not need to stay in that marriage. To solidify that thought, I rationalized that if he spoke highly of me to them and showed that I meant a lot to him, they would have taken a different approach toward me. Though the most damaging issue in the marriage was that as soon as we disagreed, he would tell me I had only married him for the benefit of staying in the country. That was the deepest hurt to my soul and the main reason for leaving him. I told myself that I could not spend the rest of my life listening to him say that, which was something he did as soon as there was a disagreement.

Regardless of all those issues, I still think to this day that he was a good man. He brought my daughter to Chicago, and before that, he ensured she was not in need of anything. He also took care of me and refused my offer to assist him financially in the home. He was very kind to me. He did not realize that the main reason for the dissolution of the marriage was his family's attitude and his belief about my reasons for marrying him.

To this day, I harbor no ill will toward him and wish him and his family all the good things in life, because I never forget the kindness he extended to me.

Prior to leaving Chicago, I had the opportunity to explore the working climate in the city. I worked at two places in the capacity of a Word Processor. Were my experiences favorable? They were, but I experienced a lot of unfriendliness from my coworkers. It was more noticeable at the second place I worked, which was a bank. The Black people would walk past without a nod or even saying hi.

I recall asking one of them, who spoke to me, I guess, because I would give her a ride to work, "Why are all these people so unfriendly? I would speak, and they don't reply."

I will never forget her response: "Well, I guess they think that you can look good some of the time, but not all the time, and you are not even from here."

I was left speechless! For I had no response to what she said. All I said to myself was, "Wow, I can't believe this."

However, I still enjoyed the bank, and my supervisors were very nice to me. Regardless of the unfriendly attitude, I was given a very nice send-off when I resigned and told them I was going back to Florida.

But before I left Chicago, the second tragedy occurred.

It was a Sunday night in October when I received a call that impacted my life for years. The lady with whom my daughter lived when I migrated to the USA, called my mother-in-law, a call that played havoc on my life for many years. The ironic thing is, she could not contact me directly, but because of the intelligence of my daughter Natalia, she was able to connect with my mother-in-law, who resided on the first floor.

So, I was called downstairs.

When I entered the house, everyone was looking at me strangely. My mother-in-law looked at me with a sad, nervous look and said, "I got a call from Jamaica…"

I immediately screamed, "My father?"

"Yes."

"Is he dead?"

"Yes."

I ran upstairs and went through the most horrible time of my life. I did not wait to hear how he died. They had to call a Priest for me and got sleeping pills, pills that reacted negatively to my body because I hallucinated that my father was choking me and telling me that I caused his death.

To this day, I have never taken another sleeping pill.

The uncanny reason why I knew my father was dead once I heard it was a call from Jamaica, because six months prior, I had been having nightmares that he was shot to death. The pain and the funeral were so real. Additionally, I experienced a pervasive sense of dread throughout the entire six months.

I later found out that political gunmen surrounded his home and stayed outside and shot into the house. Viv was shot and died immediately, but my father later died because he was not able to get to the hospital. I never dreamt of Viv's death until the last dream that I had, which was a double funeral.

Viv's death affected me too, because before my departure to the USA, we had developed a good relationship. I would send money for her, especially on her birthday. We would communicate by mail, and she would keep me abreast of what was happening during the election period. I think one of the things that helped heal our relationship was the fact that she genuinely liked my daughter, Natalia, a fact that I found surprising since she didn't like either of her parents.

I am glad that we had developed a positive relationship, despite the evilness of Jezzy, who perpetrated all sorts of malicious lies to undermine the relationship that we developed. I do remember the past, because those were the formative years of my life, and had I not been born with a fighter spirit and ambition, my life would have taken a different turn.

In retrospect, the loss of my father also contributed to my departure from Chicago. My father would not have approved of me leaving my marriage, because he was happy that I got married, and from all that he heard from me, my spouse sounded like a good man. However, I made the decision based on the culmination of everything that I had been experiencing since my arrival in Chicago.

Chicago holds a special place in my heart because I thoroughly enjoyed the city. But did I ever regret leaving? The answer is no, because without a doubt, I would not have achieved all that I have, such as a higher education, personal and financial growth, and most importantly, my second marriage that resulted in two wonderful children.

Chapter 13: My Relocation to Miami, Florida

Once I decided to move to Miami, I started to gather my things. I had them packed neatly in the hall. However, Rich thought it was a ploy because he frequently told me, "You are no fool; you are not going anywhere." He said this because I did not have any financial responsibilities—he took care of the household expenses. But regardless of that fact, I told myself that my peace of mind was better.

He found out that I was serious as a heart attack! I asked for the assistance of one of my classmates from Jamaica, who was residing in Miami. Thankfully, he and his mom came to Chicago and assisted me with the drive to Miami. Ha-ha, unfortunately, the mom thought I talked too much because I vented throughout the trip about my experiences.

Finally, I arrived in Miami in October.

Then began the process of obtaining employment. Honestly, it took only six weeks before I got a job with a huge insurance company. But prior to that, because I am a person who had no one to depend on, and being a hard worker, I took a job that was out of character for my then qualifications. I mention this because the treatment remained with me, as that was really my first experience with some sort of discrimination. The job was to be an assistant to a man who needed help getting to places, like the pharmacy, and other requirements. However, I was also to assist him with anything he needed done. Now, the bizarre part of this was his wife. She was a very impertinent person and obviously thought slavery was still in effect, or that I was so beneath them. I was only allowed to eat in their kitchen. Mind you, I was not a domestic helper; I was a certified Data Processor with at least twelve college credits. I left that job within a week or two and spent my time pursuing jobs that were more suitable, and the suitability came in the form of the job at the large insurance company.

The job at the insurance company lasted thirteen years. Overall, I enjoyed working there, and my bachelor's degree was accomplished while I was employed with this company. The sad day came when I had to hand in my resignation to complete my teaching internship that lasted three months. Fortunately, after completing my internship, I got a position as a long-term Substitute Teacher. I was observed by the Principal and other APs, resulting in good observations, which enabled me to get my first full-time teaching position at a high school. This first position was not in the county where I resided, and it was a very difficult year for me, based on a specific AP and some of the "entitled" students and their parents. Based on that experience, I decided not to return to the same school and got a job in my own county.

During the summer when school was out, I started the search for a new school to teach. As usual, I found employment quickly and landed in a school as a Language Arts/Reading Teacher and remained there for eighteen years.

I had many wonderful years teaching at the school until the last two years of my career. Unfortunately, we changed Principals, and the new one came to the school and targeted a few teachers to harass; unfortunately, I was one of them. Fortunately, she was not successful in all her attempts to get me away from the school. I later retired, but based on stupidity, I returned because she was replaced, and a few of my colleagues highly recommended me as a very good teacher. I am still wondering if my ego played a role and why I did not take the time to think logically about returning to that school. However, sixteen years out of my eighteen years were very successful, and I was rated as a very good teacher. In addition, I held leadership roles after my first year at the school. Unfortunately, this caused a lot of jealousy from colleagues. The saddest memories entailed the injustices that I suffered because some of the teachers would discuss me with students, and this led to these students creating a dislike for me, causing many lies and mischiefs to be directed at me. Another factor was the professional way I dressed. I was told by at least two teachers when I inquired about the reason for the unfriendliness from the females. Well, I was told that the way I dressed was the problem. I guess I should have switched up by looking casual sometimes.

In retrospect, teaching was my passion. I was a very kind and caring teacher; I would treat my students to treats and pizza parties as a reward for high achievements on tests. Most importantly, I would never give a child an F as a final grade because I think they did put some effort, although not the required amount. As it pertains to the relationship between my students and myself, are there things that I could do differently? The answer to this is yes! I was a no-nonsense type of teacher, where misbehaving was not tolerated. However, maybe my strategies to alleviate misbehavior could be less stern, but I also must remember that the school and the caliber of students were very challenging. But there is one thing that I am proud of and should be perceived as my legacy—my reputation as a good teacher. This reputation was earned because my students always achieved good scores on their annual standardized tests, regardless of how low they were when they entered my classes.

My memory of this era of my life is very fulfilling, and I am blessed that my oldest daughter, Natalia, has followed in my footsteps as a teacher and is doing an outstanding job. Her husband, Anthony, and my youngest sister, Aretha, are also still teaching. Ironically, I have a total of six family members who are educators.

Epilogue

It is widely believed that the first formative years of a child's life are crucial to their development. While this premise can be debated, research does suggest that early childhood experiences significantly shape emotional, cognitive, and social growth.

The irony, however, is that a child who endures a traumatic early childhood does not necessarily become a burden to society. Many go on to lead healthy, productive lives, with or without professional support. This may be attributed to innate resilience, supportive relationships later in life, or an individual's capacity for adaptation and growth.

Ultimately, while early trauma can leave lasting imprints, it does not irrevocably determine a person's destiny. An individual can build a fulfilling and meaningful life despite the shadows of a difficult childhood.

***

Upon reflection of my life up to this point, can I say that things changed for the better with the children of Viv and my father? The answer is a resounding no. It is my belief that the things their mother did to me was their karma, but could this have been broken? Yes, it could have been, if they were not as evil, ungrateful, and slanderous towards me; at least two of the six will remain non-existent to me. However, regardless of the harm they did to me, I have been able to live my life without having them be a part of it, and by God's grace, my ambition, kindness, and hard work allowed me to be abundantly blessed.

My father and Viv had six children; of the six, I have a semi-relationship with maybe three of them. I am not in a position to think that there is any real love for me from those three. However, I hold no malice in my heart for them, and I vow that I will help any of them if they are in need. My father had six children who were not mothered by Viv—four girls and two boys. Unfortunately, two of the boys are deceased. I am very proud to say that the four girls are educated professionals and are all doing well.

I have one haunting regret about my own mother's children. I understand that she had five children, and sadly, I don't know where they are. I do pray that maybe I will meet at least one of them before I leave this earth.

Finally, I have one warning that I would like to pass on to females or males, but mostly females: "If you meet someone with a child and marriage is being discussed, never marry that person if you know that you will not be able to accept that person's child. Maltreating an innocent child and treating yours with love will only bring a disastrous future for your own children."

PUT GOD FIRST IN ALL THAT YOU DO IN LIFE!

www.ingramcontent.com/pod-product-compliance
Lightning Source LLC
LaVergne TN
LVHW020638100826
845148LV00012B/2234

* 9 7 9 8 9 5 0 5 5 8 0 1 6 *